DI030930

BIOGRAPHY AND CRITICISM

General Editors
A. NORMAN JEFFARES
R. L. C. LORIMER

8

TOLSTOY THE ASCETIC

G. W. SPENCE

TOLSTOY
THE ASCETIC

BARNES & NOBLE, Inc.

NEW YORK

PUBLISHERS & BOOKSELLERS SINCE 1873

OLIVER AND BOYD LTD

TWEEDDALE COURT
EDINBURGH I

39A WELBECK STREET
LONDON W I

FIRST PUBLISHED 1967
IN GREAT BRITAIN

First published in the United States 1968
by Barnes & Noble, Inc.
New York, N.Y.

PRINTED IN GREAT BRITAIN
BY R. & R. CLARK, LIMITED

Acknowledgments

I AM deeply grateful to Sir Isaiah Berlin for the encouragement that he has given me in this work. When I sent him a copy of an essay, " Tolstoy's Dualism ", which I had written for submission to the examiners in Part II of the English Tripos at Cambridge in 1960, he urged me to have the essay published. He encouraged me the following year to continue my examination of Tolstoy's thought ; he was convinced that Tolstoy, being a precise, hard-headed thinker, was worth studying closely. On seeing my article, " Suicide and Sacrifice in Tolstoy's Ethics ", he sent me a long letter of very helpful criticism. In particular, he pointed out the need to elucidate Tolstoy's conception of God, and suggested that I should consider Schopenhauer's influence on Tolstoy. I wrote Chapter III of this book in response to that advice.

" Tolstoy's Dualism " was published in *The Russian Review*, Vol. 20, July 1961 ; " Suicide and Sacrifice in Tolstoy's Ethics " was published in Vol. 22 of the same periodical, April 1963. These articles, with considerable alterations and additions, form Chapters 1 and IV of the present work. I am grateful to the editor of *The Russian Review* for permission to have the articles thus reproduced.

Almost all the quotations from Tolstoy are taken from the translations by Louise and Aylmer Maude (Oxford University Press). The translations from Axelrod and Plekhanov are my own.

G. W. S.

Cambridge
April 1967

Contents

Introduction

AT a reception at the Great-Britain-U.S.S.R. Association, I was once rash enough to tell a Siberian doctor that I was writing a book on Tolstoy's religious philosophy. She replied flatly, "Religion was Tolstoy's mistake", expressing an opinion which she had presumably acquired at an early age, but which only after a long inquiry was proving half-true to me. I had then only recently found the criticisms of Tolstoy by the Marxists Lyubov Axelrod and Plekhanov, which appeared more than half a century ago, and which show to what barrenness and self-contradiction Tolstoy's dichotomy of the temporal and the eternal inevitably leads. But although I rejected both Tolstoy's premises and his conclusions, I could not but regard my interlocutor's comment as superficial, in view of the motives which had compelled Tolstoy to turn to the Gospels and elaborate a philosophy, and considering that one can hardly even discuss what sort of artist he would have been if he had not been obsessed with problems of a religious nature. Not only is such a religious work of art as *The Death of Ivan Ilych* a great achievement, but also *War and Peace* and *Anna Karenina* represent a search for the meaning of life, and in them the movement towards illumination is so interrelated with the fictional narrative, that the latter cannot be contemplated at any depth in isolation from the author's metaphysical quest.

This book is an analysis of Tolstoy's asceticism, not a history of it. In his early diaries and published works there are ascetic and idealistic tendencies, which have often been pointed out, so that there is ground for insisting on the essential unity of his thought throughout his life and, in spite of the contradictions with which he struggled, denying that at any point a radical change took place in him. The saintly old man in Part III of *Resurrection* is of the same type as Grisha, one of God's fools, in *Childhood*, and both are presented as subjects for admiration. But in *Childhood*:

> The emotion with which I listened to Grisha could not last long; in the first place because my curiosity was satisfied, and secondly because I had pins and needles in my legs from sitting so long in one position . . .[1]

whereas behind the unnamed saint in *Resurrection* there is a supposedly coherent philosophy of life which Nekhlyudov is obliged to accept, and which is offered as the way of salvation for all. In order to explain why Tolstoy had to *become* an ascetic, it is not enough to point to the influence on him of the beliefs and experiences of his early childhood, to his characteristic self-contempt and desire to strive for self-perfection, and to the breakdown of the ancient patriarchal relations in Russia. The main point is that in the 1870's, after the experience that he called "the Arzamas misery", he felt that life is a cheat and was in danger of killing himself, and an ascetic religion was the only means of escape from suicide. Therefore, in spite of the insistence on the unity of his thought throughout his life, it is still meaningful to speak of his "conversion" in order to describe that time when he committed himself to ascetic religion. And accordingly one may study his conversion as he himself wished us to understand it (though I have depended to some extent on a work he did not think worth publishing, *The Memoirs of a Madman*), and one may criticise the teaching that he offered in his published works after his conversion, without looking for its sources in his earliest speculations.

The starting-point of this book is not *Childhood* but *War and Peace*.

In *The Cossacks*, which was written before *War and Peace*, the hero has a choice between asceticism and a more complex attitude to life which is almost its opposite, but no final commitment is made; in *War and Peace*, on the other hand, in the minds of Prince Andrew and Pierre and in the speculation on historical determinism, a definite search for some ultimate truth is conducted, and answers are finally given.

This present book begins with consideration of the most

[1] *Childhood*, Ch. xii.

abstract side of *War and Peace*, relying heavily on Sir Isaiah Berlin's *The Hedgehog and the Fox*. In view of the fact that, as Sir Isaiah Berlin says, little attempt has been made in the past to relate Tolstoy's theory of history to his subsequent thought, I have now tried to do so. My first chapter is an attempt to relate his theory of history and of freedom and inevitability to those later works—the *Confession, On Life,* and parts of *The Kingdom of God is Within You*—in which he expresses what he believes to be the basic metaphysical truth of Christianity. A comparison of the dualism in *War and Peace* of historical determinism and consciousness of freedom with the dualism in the later essays of the animal and the rational or divine elements in man, will show how the theory of history supports the ideal of non-resistance to evil.

Parallel to the abstract speculation in *War and Peace* are more intimate searches for truth carried on by Prince Andrew and Pierre. To follow those searches and examine their results, with some understanding of Tolstoy's metaphysics, and of his attempt to transcend his own determinism, already in our minds, will show how one search issues in characteristic Tolstoyan dualism, and the other in a rival belief. Although Andrew's final insight is one you can die with but not live with, it is his answer rather than Pierre's which was to save Tolstoy. "To live rationally one must live so that death cannot destroy life." Pierre's idea of God as immanent is vague and inadequate.

A study of Pierre and Andrew leads on to one of Levin, and of Tolstoy's own spiritual crisis. In discussing the latter I am not aiming at biography, nor am I concerned with the possible social, psychological, and physiological causes of the crisis so much as with Tolstoy's own interpretation of it. One can, indeed, speculate endlessly on the causes of "the Arzamas misery", as one can, equally, on the later psychological disorder that must lie behind his anti-sex sermon. But just as, when I consider *The Kreutzer Sonata* in Chapter iv, I only look at how it is logically connected with his metaphysics, so in Chapter ii my subject is Tolstoy's interpretation of his crisis, for it is an interpretation in terms of dualism, related, therefore, to *War and Peace* and forming the basis of his religious teaching.

The Death of Ivan Ilych, *The Power of Darkness*, and *Master and Man* are considered next, because, besides being ethical works reflecting his metaphysics, they are tragedies that explore what he called the intrinsic contradiction of life, and that thus present (in the most concentrated and accomplished form) his understanding of what was in essence his own spiritual crisis.

The metaphysical system which he felt compelled to formulate from his awareness of this contradiction, and argued at length in the essay *On Life*, is examined in Chapter III. Some knowledge of this essay is essential to a correct understanding of Tolstoy's teaching. Although it is muddled, obscure and dogmatic, it represents his attempt to express his beliefs as a rational philosophy. The inadequacy of this attempt meant that he had, in his moralising, to rely on a conception of the will of God which his metaphysics do not warrant. Holding that for all men the good of animal existence is equal to zero, and yet rejecting suicide, he believed that man's animal existence has been given by God to be used solely as an instrument in the fulfilment of God's purpose.

An examination in Chapter IV of the ideals of non-resistance to evil and of complete celibacy shows that, although Tolstoy's ascetic religion served as a means of overcoming the temptation of suicide, it leads inevitably to a denial of what is usually understood by life.

Chapter V is a criticism of Dr George Steiner's attempt to associate Tolstoy with the Grand Inquisitor in *The Brothers Karamazov*, and with the Communists. This attempt is wrongheaded, because Dr Steiner has failed to appreciate Tolstoy's dualism and the life-denying nature of his ethical system. My contention is that, although Tolstoy sometimes spoke of the Kingdom of God on earth, the idea of it is logically incompatible with his doctrinal principles, and that these principles are fundamentally opposed to those of Dostoevsky's Inquisitor and of the Communists.

Finally there is an appreciation of *Resurrection*. As it is sometimes underrated, I have tried to point out some of its artistic merits. But I have also considered it as what it manifestly is: another expression of its author's dualism. It is a revelation of his final world-view, and its basic weakness is the weakness of that world-view.

This, then, is a moral and philosophical valuation of Tolstoy, looking at him not so much in his historical context as in his rôle of a seeker after truth and a teacher of what he thought were eternal truths, and singling out those aspects of his artistic creation that are most relevant to that rôle.

I

Dualism

1 Inevitability and Freedom

IT is tempting to skip most of the philosophical dissertations in *War and Peace,* for they strike one from the outset as being heavy-going and not satisfactorily integrated into the structure of the work as a whole. The accusatory question is often asked: If Tolstoy can adequately suggest in artistic terms the significance of Kutuzov and the insignificance of Napoleon, why does he get the bit between his teeth and laboriously argue a case for historical determinism? Or why does he, in the narrative parts, deliberately belittle Napoleon, and play down Kutuzov's faults and exaggerate his virtues? *The Hedgehog and the Fox* is a brilliant and well-known study of Tolstoy's theory of history; Sir Isaiah Berlin has no difficulty in showing that the theory deserves to be taken seriously. Pointing to Tolstoy's distortion of facts, and not attempting to justify the place of abstract argument in a work of art, he considers the importance of the central thesis in *War and Peace* and its relation to the descriptions of the personal lives of men and women, their thoughts, passions, and activities. But he is examining Tolstoy's attitude to history, he says, "for the light it casts on a single man of genius rather than on the fate of all mankind". He reveals a fundamental psychological conflict by exploring the inconsistency between Tolstoy's talent and opinions. The following paragraphs contain a summary of Tolstoy's theory of history and inevitability, but only to use it as a point of departure. Interesting as are the questions why he wanted a theory of history, and why he adopted a kind of determinism, the point to be made here is that Tolstoy, feeling that the consciousness of freely exercising choice is essential to life, found in the end that he could not accept the complete determinism towards which his argument seemed to be leading. The

I

question arises whether his conclusion consists in saying that, although we are the objects of a complete causal determinism, we shall never experience full awareness of this and shall retain an illusory consciousness of free will even though it can be proved that we have in fact no freedom at all; or whether he thought that he could transcend his determinism without contradicting anything he had said before, and so grant that we have a limited degree of real freedom. It is claimed here that the latter is the case, but that, although he thought that consciousness of freedom is not illusory, he could not see how a man's consciousness of freedom could modify his actions, or be anything but a constant vital force, so that he was driven into believing in the co-existence of two distinct realms: the realm of events subject to time and space and in dependence on cause, and an obscure realm of metaphysical freedom.

But first the case for determinism: *War and Peace* was called by Kareyev "a historical poem on the philosophical theme of duality",[1] and this description is substantiated in particular by the comments Tolstoy makes in Volume III, Part I, Chapter I, where he opens his philosophic argument:

> There are two sides to the life of every man, his individual life which is the more free the more abstract its interests, and his elemental swarm-life in which he inevitably obeys laws laid down for him.
>
> Man lives consciously for himself, but is an unconscious instrument in the attainment of the historic, universal, aims of humanity.

The novel shows that what is most real to Tolstoy as an artist lies in the actions and sensations of the individual characters, the passions and play of feeling between persons, the daily lives of people living for themselves. But at the same time he is tormented by the questions that torment Pierre Bezukhov: "What for?" and "Why?" As a thinker Tolstoy is not content to look at the emotions and actions of his characters for what they are in themselves, but must relate them to a wider vision of the life of humanity, in which he hopes to find their significance. As Sir Isaiah Berlin points out, the arguments about the interpretation of history are not merely an

---

[1] Quoted by Sir Isaiah Berlin in *The Hedgehog and the Fox*, III, p. 53.

attempt to define the historian's task, but constitute a search for some "universal explanatory principle", in the light of which the specific and diverse qualities of individual lives may be understood.[2]

Tolstoy must know in the first place why the French invasion of Russia took place at all; why the French made every effort to push on to Moscow at a time when doing so was bound to lead to disaster; and why the Russians did not think of luring Napoleon on into the depths of their country, and yet did so quite fortuitously.

We are forced to fall back on fatalism as an explanation of irrational events (that is to say, events the reasonableness of which we do not understand). The more we try to explain such events in history reasonably, the more unreasonable and incomprehensible do they become to us.

This use of the word "fatalism" is in part rhetorical, but Tolstoy's tendency to speak and think as a fatalist obscures his discussion of scientific determinism. Wanting to find a universal explanatory principle, he is not concerned, as J. S. Mill, for example, was, about the possibility of there being a real distinction between determinism and fatalism or irresistibility. For rather than saying that human actions take place by necessity, which may suggest that nothing can be done to counteract a powerful tendency, a determinist, if he is not also a fatalist, should confine himself to the statement that human actions are consequent on causes. Perhaps then Tolstoy's words *"neobkhodimost'"* and *"neizbezhnost'"*, which mean "necessity" and "inevitability", have misleading associations; for it is consistent with determinism to say that a motive may be resisted and overcome, that the action which would result from it may be avoided, and that man exercises choice—but the choice is not "free": though it is not constrained, it is certainly determined by some cause. And if these words have misleading associations, it is very likely that Tolstoy was misled by them. For, as will be shown in due course, there comes a time when, having apparently found an explanatory principle, he is distressed by the iron laws of necessity which it seems to involve.

Complaining that the term "chance" explains nothing, and

[2] *The Hedgehog and the Fox*, III, p. 58.

finding the notion that the "genius" of leaders is the cause of events to be particularly objectionable—in any case, historians cannot say wherein the genius of leaders consists—,[3] he produces his famous simile of the rams, which betrays a powerful tendency to think as a fatalist.

> To a herd of rams, the ram the herdsman drives each evening into a special enclosure to feed, and that becomes twice as fat as the others, must seem to be a genius. And it must appear an astonishing conjunction of genius with a whole series of extraordinary chances that this ram, who instead of getting into the general fold every evening gets into a special enclosure where there are oats—this very ram, swelling with fat, is killed for meat.
>
> But the rams need only cease to suppose that all that happens to them happens solely for the attainment of their sheepish aims, they need only admit that what happens to them may also have purposes beyond their ken, and they will at once perceive a unity and coherence in what happened to the ram that was fattened. Even if they do not know for what purpose they are fattened, they will at least know that all that happened to the ram did not happen accidentally, and will no longer need the conceptions of *chance* or *genius*.

Not only can the rams not resist the herdsman, but it is assumed that the understanding of causes entails the acknowledgment of a unity ("*yedinstvo*") in history which is dependent on some mysterious ultimate purpose; teleology is confused with a discussion of antecedent causes.

In trying to answer the question asked in the Epilogue, Part II: "What force moves the nations?" Tolstoy finds that there are historians of three sorts. Those of one sort attribute, say, the campaign of 1813 and the restoration of the Bourbons to the will of Alexander. But Gervinus, who is an example of another sort of historian, refuting this narrow view, tries to prove that these events were due to other things as well: the activities of Metternich, Madame de Staël, Talleyrand, Fichte, Chateaubriand and others. But the sum of these component forces—that is, the interaction of these people—does not equal the resultant, namely the phenomenon of millions of Frenchmen

[3] *War and Peace*, Epilogue, Part I, Chs. II-IV.

submitting to the Bourbons; so that, to explain how the submission of millions of people resulted from the mutual relations of a few, Gervinus is obliged to assume an unexplained force—power—acting on the resultant. Historians of a third kind maintain that the cause of events lies in intellectual activity. But how the *Contrat Social* had the effect of making Frenchmen drown one another, cannot be understood without an explanation of the causal nexus of an idea with an event. An idea is only one more component force. Indeed, as soon as historians of culture come to describe a particular historical event, they involuntarily resort to the concept of power; they say, for instance, that the campaign of 1812 was the work of Napoleon's will.

What, then, is power? What was the ground of Napoleon's power? He could not, in the manner of Hercules, threaten to use direct physical force against weaker beings, since the implementing of his threats would depend on the co-operation of numerous other men. Nor was his power based on the predominance of moral strength, for he had none; and even if we suppose that he did have special moral strength or genius, we cannot on such a basis account for the fact that Louis XI and Metternich, for example, appeared, like Napoleon, to rule over millions of people, although they were morally weaker than most of their subjects. Do rulers, then, have power because the collective will of the people is invested in them? Tolstoy goes to some lengths to demolish this theory, which, he says, may be a useful fiction in jurisprudence but can tell us nothing about actual events. There is no need to reproduce his discussion of the different ways in which this theory can be understood; it is enough to quote the conclusion to this part of his argument:

> What causes historical events? Power. What is power? Power is the collective will of the people transferred to one person. Under what condition is the will of the people delegated to one person? On condition that that person expresses the will of the whole people. That is, power is power: in other words, power is a word the meaning of which we do not understand.

It is evident from the standpoint of experience, however, that power is "merely the relation that exists between the expression of someone's will and the execution of that will by others". For how was it that Napoleon's commands for an invasion of England were ignored, and not those for an invasion of Russia? Evidently the execution of his commands depended on certain conditions over which he had no control. Those commands which were inconsistent with the course of events that was already developing remained unexecuted.[4]

And so Tolstoy arrives at what Sir Isaiah Berlin calls

> one of his celebrated paradoxes: the higher soldiers or states-men are in the pyramid of authority, the farther they must be from its base which consists of those ordinary men and women whose lives are the actual stuff of history; and, consequently, the smaller the effect of the words and acts of such remote personages, despite all their theoretical authority, upon that history.[5]

In Tolstoy's words, "A king is history's slave".

There can be little doubt that here, as elsewhere, Tolstoy exaggerates. He is anxious to controvert an extreme point of view, that the wills of certain individuals are all-powerful, and that men like Napoleon make history. But his own view is just as extravagant: that individuals, at least in their social, if not in their private lives, are totally powerless, and that history makes itself, the so-called great men being mere labels for events which would have taken place nonetheless without them.

But he does not leave the argument there. He is trying not merely to demolish the reputations of "great" men, but to consider history as a science. For if it is a science, it must be possible to discover and formulate a set of laws of history, by which we should be able to predict the future in human affairs as certainly as we can in astronomy. But all those who have attempted a science of history have arbitrarily selected their material and arbitrarily emphasised certain tendencies, whether political or cultural, so that what they examine is only a small fraction of what actually constitutes history. A correct historical science could only operate by doing the im-possible: that is, by taking everything into consideration and

---

[4] *War and Peace*, Epilogue, Part II, Chs. II-VII.
[5] *The Hedgehog and the Fox*, III, p. 30.

making no selection. We cannot arrive at a true understanding of history if we study the lives only of the Caesars, Alexanders, Luthers and Voltaires, and not of all, absolutely all those who take part in an event. Moreover, the movement of humanity is continuous; we must not arbitrarily select a certain series of events: "there is and can be no *beginning* to any event, for one event always flows uninterruptedly from another". For a correct historical science, we should need to study not smaller and smaller units in the motion of history, but "the common, infinitesimally small elements by which the masses are moved".[6]

For it is not only that the motion of history arises from innumerable human wills, but also that any action is conditioned by circumstances and dependent on a cause or complex of causes. The question thus arises whether we have any free will at all. Our actions seem to be the result of our free will only when we do not know by what they are conditioned or caused, but the more we know of the circumstances of an action, the less degree of free will do we ascribe to it. To conceive of a man having perfect freedom, we must imagine that he is outside of space and time and free from dependence on cause; and that is impossible. To conceive of "the action of a man entirely subject to the law of inevitability, without any freedom, we must assume the knowledge of an *infinite* number of space relations, an *infinitely* long period of time, and an *infinite* series of causes." That is, we must know *all* the circumstances in which the action was performed, and all the influences acting on the agent; and we must know not only the causes of the action but the causes of those causes, and so on to infinity. And, fortunately, all this, too, is impossible. Besides, "as soon as there is no freedom there is also no man".

If the ideal historical science were possible, that is, if we could "observe" the infinitely small elements that determine the motion of history (Tolstoy does not say that the infinitely small equals zero), and if we could so integrate them as to be able to arrive at the laws of history, the possibility of life, he says, would be destroyed. For life is a spontaneous activity involving consciousness of free will, and, if we reached a conception of complete inevitability, we should deprive ourselves

[6] *War and Peace*, Vol. III, Part III, Ch. I.

of such life.[7] But Tolstoy seems at times to say that the inexorable laws of history are nevertheless working themselves out,
and that it is only our necessary ignorance of them which
creates the illusion of free will. As Sir Isaiah Berlin interprets
his arguments, "the reality of inexorable historical determinism
[is] not, indeed, experienced directly, but [is] known to be true
on irrefutable theoretical grounds".

And Sir Isaiah Berlin explains that, if this is the case, then
the life of the Rostovs, Bolkonskis, and others—that "moral life
with its sense of responsibility, joys, sorrows, sense of guilt and
sense of achievement"—is a vast illusion. Tolstoy's thesis consists in contrasting the "delusive experience of free will, the
feeling of responsibility, the values of private life generally",
with a real and inexorable necessity. Although, in comparison
with the abstractions of scientists and historians that he scorn-
fully denounces, personal experience and concrete individual
life appear to present a superior reality, yet, because there is
no free will, everything being governed by laws, that experience
and that life remain a mere illusion. There is thus an unre-
solved conflict in Tolstoy, which is mirrored by another: the
conflict within him "between instinctive judgment and theoretical conviction—between his gifts and his opinions"; and
out of these contradictions the novel grew.[8]

It is evident that Tolstoy made the assumption (and Sir
Isaiah Berlin follows him in this[9]) that any form of genuine
determinism entails the elimination of the notion of individual
responsibility. But this proposition is doubtful. The conception of individual responsibility implies that one's choices are
one's own and that one could, on a given occasion, have done
something other than what one actually did—that is to say,
that one would have acted differently if, the external circumstances being the same, one's judgment of them or one's preferences at the time had not been what they were. And we can
say that the characters in *War and Peace* have a belief in their
own responsibility, without asserting that they have the experi-

---

[7] *War and Peace*, Epilogue, Part II, Chs. VIII-x.

[8] *The Hedgehog and the Fox*, III, pp. 47-8 and 65.

[9] *Historical Inevitability*, Auguste Comte Memorial Trust Lecture, 12 May 1953,
p. 25. London (Oxford University Press), 1954.

ence—whether illusory or not—of "free will". We can say that such a belief is true, without asserting that, to be one's own, a choice or its cause must not be completely determined by causes.

But Tolstoy, as has been seen, was not merely a determinist who thought that all events, including volitions, have antecedent causes. He tended to think as a fatalist; and if our actions are made to conform to the necessities of some pattern that is as incomprehensible to us as the will of the herdsman was to the rams, then the sense of personal responsibility that we have really is illusory. So far, then, Sir Isaiah Berlin is right: he sees Tolstoy as a kind of fatalist, who thinks that the data of experience must belong to a system, involving an ultimate purpose; and Tolstoy, not seeing that there is any possibility that the logic of his argument might lead him to a form of determinism with which belief in personal responsibility may be quite compatible, jumps to the conclusion that, if a man's volitions are fully determined by causes, he has no life. As this conclusion is intolerable, he has to find a way out. And here, it seems, Sir Isaiah Berlin's explanation is not complete; for not even in *War and Peace* did Tolstoy hold that we shall always retain, and be able to live by, a merely illusory consciousness of free will, but he declares even there that such a consciousness is real, and to show that it is warranted he produces a metaphysical argument taken, as the Russian critic Eykhenbaum has pointed out, from Schopenhauer.[10]

The reality of consciousness of freedom is asserted in the Epilogue, Part II, first in Chapter VIII and again in Chapter X. In the former chapter Tolstoy says:

> The problem is, that regarding man as a subject of observation from whatever point of view—theological, historical, ethical, or philosophic—we find a general law of necessity to which he (like all that exists) is subject. But regarding him from within ourselves, as what we are conscious of, we feel ourselves to be free.
> This consciousness is a source of self-cognition quite apart

[10] B. M. Eykhenbaum, *Lev Tolstoy, the 1870's*, ed. B. I. Bursov, Part II, Ch. 2, pp. 109-115. Eykhenbaum refers to Schopenhauer's essay *On the Freedom of the Will*.

from and independent of reason. Through his reason man ob-
serves himself, but only through consciousness does he know
himself.

This Schopenhauerian distinction between knowledge and
observation was to play an important part in Tolstoy's thought.
In a passage which anticipates the introductory theme of the
religious essay *On Life*, writers who, on the basis of scientific
discoveries, deny the existence of the soul and freedom are
denounced as ignoramuses. Tolstoy here adopts Schopenhauer's opinion that a man becomes directly conscious of himself as a living being by the fact that he wills, thus adumbrating
his subsequent definition of life as "the striving after good".
In Chapter x, following the statement that the conceptions of
perfect freedom and of complete inevitability are both impossible, Tolstoy writes:

> Reason says: (1) Space with all the forms of matter that give
> it visibility is infinite and cannot be imagined otherwise. (2)
> Time is infinite motion without a moment of rest and is un-
> thinkable otherwise. (3) The connexion between cause and
> effect has no beginning and can have no end.
> Consciousness says: (1) I alone am, and all that exists is
> but me, consequently I include space. (2) I measure flowing
> time by the fixed moment of the present, in which alone I am
> conscious of myself as living, consequently I am outside time.
> (3) I am beyond cause, for I feel myself to be the cause of every
> manifestation of my life.
> Reason gives expression to the laws of inevitability. Con-
> sciousness gives expression to the essence of freedom.
> Freedom not limited by anything is the essence of life in
> man's consciousness. Inevitability without content is man's
> reason in its three forms.
> Freedom is the thing examined. Inevitability is what ex-
> amines. Freedom is the content. Inevitability is the form.
> Only by separating the two sources of cognition, related to
> one another as form to content, do we get the mutually ex-
> clusive and separately incomprehensible conceptions of freedom
> and inevitability.
> Only by uniting them do we get a clear conception of man's
> life.

Apart from these two concepts which in their union mutually define one another as form and content, no conception of life is possible.

All that we know of the life of man is merely a certain relation of freewill to inevitability, that is, of consciousness to the laws of reason.

All that we know of the external world of nature is only a certain relation of the forces of nature to inevitability, or of the essence of life to the laws of reason.

The great natural forces (*rather,* The forces of life in nature) lie outside us and we are not conscious of them: we call those forces gravitation, inertia, electricity, animal force, and so on, but we are conscious of the force of life in man and we call it freedom.

It should be noted how the solipsism attributed to consciousness is qualified in the context, but it is hard to gauge the extent of the qualification that is intended. The problem is how to unite the two sources of cognition. This is the problem with which Schopenhauer was faced when he took over Kant's distinction between empirical and "intelligible" character. Postulating causality as the general law to which all objects of the external world are subject without exception, Schopenhauer maintained that the intelligible character, which is the will and is the basis of the empirical character, is independent of time, space and causality, the necessity of an action co-existing with its transcendental freedom; in itself and outside of appearance, the will is free.[11] As Patrick Gardiner has said, Schopenhauer's conception of the way in which human beings can be regarded from two distinct standpoints diverged from Kant's, one difference being that, whereas Kant believed that, since the nature of things-in-themselves is unknowable, we can never *know* ourselves to be free agents belonging to the "intelligible world", Schopenhauer claimed that we do in fact have that knowledge.[12] Tolstoy follows Schopenhauer; but while the latter insisted on the unity of body and will, Tolstoy, as will be seen, comes to adopt a fundamentally dualistic view of human nature.

[11] *On the Freedom of the Will,* Chs. III and V, translated by K. Kolenda. New York (Liberal Arts Press), 1960.
[12] *Schopenhauer,* Ch. II, pp. 57-8. Harmondsworth (Penguin) 1963.

It will be noted, too, that Tolstoy here takes over Schopenhauer's conception of the "forces of nature".[13] Like the force of gravitation, he says, the force of freedom is incomprehensible in itself, and is only understood by us in so far as we are acquainted with the laws of inevitability to which it is subject in its manifestation. The manifestation of this force of freedom, in human beings in space and time and in dependence on cause, is the subject of history. Like "vital force" in biology, freedom in history is an expression for what is still inexplicable, and would remain inexplicable even if science were to reveal all the laws of the phenomena in question. And yet this freedom is not capable of influencing the way in which historical events occur, for if it were, it would not be subject to laws in its manifestation; if one free action is ever performed, "then not a single historical law can exist, nor any conception of historical events".[14]

By this stage in the argument Tolstoy has actually dropped the word "will" and no longer speaks of the freedom of the will ("*svoboda voli*") but of freedom. It would at first sight seem strange to call the inner freedom of which we are conscious "free will", if our actions can only be regarded as the results of our freedom in so far as they are manifestations of the free force of life, when the *kind* of actions we perform is determined by conditions and causes we cannot control. The freedom, however, of which Tolstoy is speaking is not that of the faculty by which we choose between different courses of action, but that of the will as the thing-in-itself. Tolstoy seems to be saying: "I am free because I am alive, for my manifestation in time and space is a manifestation of the essence of life, which is free. But I am not free to decide how my existence shall be arranged, or even what I shall do."

As a last attempt to interpret the theory of freedom and inevitability that appears at the close of *War and Peace*, we may say: When a man performs an action, his action is affected by countless circumstances, and his motives are determined by countless causes (the nature of his impulses and desires as they

---

[13] *The World as Will and Idea*, Book II. For a discussion of this conception see Gardiner, *Schopenhauer*, Ch. IV, pp. 134-140.

[14] *War and Peace*, Epilogue, Part II, Chs. X and XI.

have come down to him and been shaped by education and environment, his previous deliberations and reflections, and all the various influences acting upon him); and yet at the same time he feels, rightly, that he is a free being and that any action which he performs is an expression of his freedom; but he is mistaken if he thinks he is free to choose to do or to forbear, to act either in accordance with one set of motives or in accordance with another, for a free choice is one that has no antecedent cause, and there must be some cause determining his choice. Yet again, to make a choice is to perform a mental action; we must be alive to choose, and we must be free to be alive, so that in the act of choice our freedom is manifest. The difficulty is due to the proposition that freedom is subject to laws in its manifestation; yet it is only by a correct understanding of this proposition that we can unite the two sources of cognition, reason and consciousness.

2 *The Animal and the Divine*

War and Peace was completed in 1869, and ten years later Tolstoy wrote his *Confession*, in which he describes how in the 1870's he was afflicted by despair as by a disease, but eventually saved himself from the temptation of suicide by conversion to Christianity. This Christianity was not the teaching of any of the churches. Indeed, when he turned to the Orthodox Church after having, as he believed, found the way of approach to God, he was so disgusted by its practices and doctrine that he felt he was drawing near to another abyss. He envied the peasants their simple faith, but could not accept the dogmas, sacraments and so on, of the church to which they belonged. It was as if he had been given some jewels in a bag of stinking dirt. Feeling like the thief on the cross who believed and was saved, he yet had a strong Voltairean element in his mind and maliciously attacked whatever seemed to him irrational or mystical. Mysticism with Tolstoy is always a subject for contempt; as for reason, the word is protean, but few dogmas withstood his critical intelligence. He appealed to common sense. In 1880 he wrote a devastating *Criticism of Dogmatic Theology*; and, anxious to find in clear, indisputable terms the saving truth of Jesus's teaching and, at the same time, to prove the claims of the Orthodox Church to be quite unfounded, he composed an impatient and unscholarly *Harmony and Translation of the Four Gospels*.

Besides showing where he differed from the priests, he had to establish a rational theology of his own, and belabour the scientific materialists. His thought is profoundly ethical: he demands guidance in life. As will be shown in Chapter II, his desire to devote himself to God is the result of the need to overcome death; and overcoming death means willingly sacrificing the life that death will destroy. He must, moreover, believe that what he is sacrificing has no value in itself, and that that for the sake of which the sacrifice is made, is real. Thus it is necessary not only to refute materialism, but also to declare a moral law based on a belief in God and immortality and in the co-existence of two distinct realms: that of organic and inorganic activity, which is only instrumental in life (as we should realise if we properly understood the concept of life), and that of consciousness and the self, where true life resides.

Tolstoy's attacks on the churches are not discussed in this work. The present section summarises his metaphysical and ethical system. Ideas and problems which are touched on here are analysed and discussed in Chapters III and IV. The purpose of this section is to introduce to the reader the main ideas of Tolstoy's last, religious period, so that he may at once understand in what sense Tolstoy's system is dualistic, and appreciate the relation between this religious dualism and the early dualism of consciousness and reason, with which *War and Peace* ended.

Tolstoy, then, in the 1870's, before his conversion, was tormented by despair. It was like a disease, the chief sympton of which was a perpetually nagging question: "What is it for? What does it lead to? . . . Why should I live? . . . Is there any meaning in my life that the inevitable death awaiting me does not destroy?" [15] These are like the questions that Pierre Bezukhov asks himself. Tolstoy was drawn towards suicide by a growing awareness of the vanity of life, which caused him to accept the conclusions of Buddha, Schopenhauer, and the author of *Ecclesiastes*; but the acceptance was only temporary;

[15] *Confession*, III and v.

he did not abandon the search for the meaning of life, which was a search for God.

The *Confession* is a passionate piece of writing; but there is no need yet to discuss the inward aspect of his search for God. The *Confession* also contains an amount of abstract thought: an essay on the range and limits of science and metaphysics, and an argument about the finite and the infinite. It is a conception of the infinite that was required to give theoretical justification to Tolstoy's newly-found religion; indeed, the idea of man's having access to an infinite realm that is outside time and space, is the essence of the matter.

For he came to understand that, when he was asking the meaning of life, he was demanding "an explanation of the finite in terms of the infinite". He had asked: "What is the meaning of my life, beyond time, cause, and space?" And the question he had replied to, when he concluded that life is senseless, was: "What is the meaning of my life within time, cause, and space?" To argue that life is meaningless, is like working on an identity when you think you are solving an equation: your labour ends with the proposition that $x = x$. Only something outside life can give it meaning; if we think of life as what goes on in time and space, to find its meaning we must refer it to something which is beyond time and space. Science, rational knowledge, cannot do this; we must appeal to faith. Only faith supplies an answer to the question Tolstoy was really asking, for faith relates our finite so-called lives to the infinite. "What am I?" he asks—"A part of the infinite. In those few words lies the whole problem." If one does not realise that, one's reasoning turns in a vicious circle.

The word "infinite" ("*beskonechny*") is used with two meanings. Here in Chapter ix of the *Confession*, it is consoling to know that one is a part of the infinite in the sense of participating in a domain that is outside time and space, whereas in Chapter vi it was found that to see oneself as a part of the infinite in the sense of being a product, doomed to extinction, of an endless material process occupying time and space, is a source of despair.

In *War and Peace* Tolstoy could escape from a theory that seemed to deny life as we know it, by asserting that the freedom

of which we are conscious is the essence of life and is not, as
an essence, subject to any law, known or unknown. In his
Confession he escapes from the conclusion that in the face of
decay and death life is but a senseless and stupid joke, by claiming that it is not the fortuitous result of the mutations of atoms,
thrown up at a particular period in endless time and on a
particular sphere in endless space, and conditioned by countless
causes, but that "God is life",[16] and that man in his inner
consciousness has a certain relationship to that infinite
God.

This point is developed in the essay *On Life*. Here Tolstoy
begins by considering the definitions of life put forward by
thinkers who base their philosophy on the results of scientific
discovery. Such a definition is this: "Life is a particular
activity of an organic substance." But he rejects these definitions on the grounds that they are in fact merely descriptions
of the sensible processes that accompany life. Experimental
science is concerned only with external phenomena, whereas
the chief characteristics of life are inner qualities: "A consciousness of suffering and enjoyment and an aspiration towards
welfare." [17] So life can be defined as "the striving after good"
("*stremlenie k blagu*"); an alternative translation would be
"striving towards welfare" or "well-being". At this early stage
in the essay it is not said in what the good or well-being consists, and the fact that different people have different conceptions of good does not destroy the definition, but is relevant to
a distinction that is made later between "animal life" and
"human life". The present definition of life can be expanded
thus: "a striving after good for oneself as a being distinct from
all the rest of the world".[18]

On this basis the distinction is again made between knowledge and observation: to observe objects, and to define them
as they are manifest to us in time and space, is not to know them;
for we only really know inner qualities: "man does not know
anything apart from his ego". At this point in the argument a
leap is taken, for the ego is regarded as being outside time and

---

[16] *Confession*, xii. See Chapter ii, section 6.
[17] *On Life*, Introduction.
[18] *Ibid.*, iv and Appendix i.

space, though it is not argued with Kant that time and space are only forms of *Anschauung*:[19] when a man

> asks himself about his place in time and space it seems to him at first that he stands in the midst of infinite time extending in both directions, and that he is the centre of a sphere whose surface is everywhere and nowhere. And it is just this self outside of time and space that a man really knows.[20]

The subsequent argument of the essay is based on this dogmatic assertion. The real self appears to be identical with what is called "reasonable consciousness" ("*razumnoe soznanie*"). Consciousness, of course—it is argued—changes moment by moment, just as the cells of the body change continuously; but there is that which unites the whole series of my consecutive consciousnesses into one, and is my real and actual self ("*nasto-yashchee i deystvitel' noe ya*"). "I know myself as that fundamental attribute", and it determines my relation to the world.[21]

Thus Tolstoy's basic religious doctrine is a development of the tentative dualism of the close of *War and Peace*. In both *On Life* and the Epilogue, Part II, the essence of life is identified with consciousness; and consciousness, reasonable consciousness or the self, is beyond the reach of cause. The word "reason" in *On Life* is used synonymously with "reasonable consciousness", whereas the discursive "reason" of the close of *War and Peace* is concerned only with phenomena and corresponds to the "observation" of the later essay.

[19] Although it is not stated in the essay *On Life* that time and space are only forms of intuition, yet presumably Tolstoy spoke so readily of a realm outside of time and space thanks to his knowledge of Kant and Schopenhauer. In his diary for 19 January 1904 we find this:
"That time and space do not exist in themselves, but are only necessary forms of thought due to our separateness, is proved by the fact that space and time are mutually defined: space is the possibility of conceiving (perceiving) two objects at one and the same time, or in general of perceiving two objects (independent of time). Time is the possibility of conceiving, perceiving two objects in one and the same space or independent of space."
[20] *On Life*, XII. Note the expression taken from Pascal, who said that space is an infinite sphere, the centre of which is everywhere, the circumference nowhere. Tolstoy passes too easily from "seems" to "really knows". See also Chapter III, section 4.
[21] *Ibid.*, XXVIII. This brief statement of the dogma is enough for the purposes of this chapter. The argument used to support it is discussed in Chapter III, section 3.

In *War and Peace* Tolstoy says that in his individual life man lives consciously for himself, and therefore man's "elemental swarm-life" must be the result of the accumulation of the wills of countless people each of whom is living for himself. To use the language of the later essay, the good for which people strive is the attainment of personal well-being, or the well-being of their families or nations, or the fulfilment of the will of their leaders. It seemed inconceivable that men should direct their energy towards any other goal than the good of themselves or of the group to which they belong, so that the result of their striving is war and the general surrender of personal responsibility that is necessitated by collective action.

Similarly in the essay *On Life*, when Tolstoy considers the consequences of a man's living for his own good, he claims that, if a man does so, he is bound to find that his personal well-being "is not merely a thing not easy of attainment, but is something that will certainly be taken from him". This is so because of the conflict he will be brought into with others, the sense of weariness, satiety and suffering, and the facts of decay and physical death. Belief in personal well-being as the spring of action is inevitably followed by disbelief in everything; and a man cannot live for his family, his country, or even for humanity as a whole, if he feels his own life to be a senseless evil.

> If my individual life is calamitous and senseless, every other human personality is equally senseless, and an infinite number of senseless and irrational personalities will not form a single good and reasonable life.[22]

The argument of the essay consists in making generalisations about life that are derived from Tolstoy's interpretation of his own experience, and in combining them with a metaphysical dogma, from which a moral law and a theory of immortality are deduced. On the other hand, his attack on the application of biological concepts to ethics is a good one; it is supported by a theory of a hierarchy of levels of activity—inorganic, organic, and psychic — and of the discontinuity between these levels, which involves a denial of the possibility of reducing ethical questions to the domain of the struggle for

[22] *On Life*, I and VI.

existence. But it is this belief in the discontinuity between levels of organisation which Tolstoy thinks entitles him to dogmatise about a realm outside time and space, and to announce a dualistic conception of human nature that is as naïve as the old dualism of body and soul. He divides man into "reasonable consciousness" and "animal personality" ("*zhivotnaya lichnost'* "). To live for one's personal well-being is to live for the sake of the animal personality; and, as animals, in the struggle for existence, strive only for the survival of themselves and of their whelps and herd, so, if a man's feeling for his own whelps or herd—his family or nation—includes a preference for his whelps or herd to others, then that so-called love, it is said, is not love at all but merely a preference based on personal interest, since the life and welfare of family and nation contribute to one's personal well-being.[23] And—it is argued in *The Kingdom of God is Within You*—the love for the whole of humanity taught by Positivists and others is also impossible; for love for family or nation cannot be extended, as they would like, to the whole of humanity, as there are no inner motives for such an extension, however necessary or advantageous it may appear to be when one thinks about it. Therefore, unless the demands of reasonable consciousness are recognised, only preferences, not real love, and animal life are possible. "Human", as opposed to animal, "life begins only with the appearance of a reasonable consciousness—the very thing that . . . produces in [man] the negation of the good of the personal life." [24] For, whereas conflict, weariness, satiety, suffering, decay, and death destroy personal life, it is reason that makes one aware of the certainty of that destruction, and torments one to the point of suicide.

Recognition of the demands of reasonable consciousness is a gradual process, but it can be summed up in the Greek word "*metanoia*". A quotation from *The Kingdom of God is Within You* will show what Tolstoy understood by this word:

> Understand that this corporeal personal life which is here to-day and is destroyed to-morrow, can have no permanence, that no external measures, no arrangement of it, can give it firmness or

[23] *Ibid.*, xxiii.   [24] *Ibid.*, vii.

C

make it rational. Bethink yourselves, and understand that the life you are living is not true life; the life of the family, of society, of the state, will not save you from destruction. A true, rational life is possible for man only in the measure to which he can participate, not in the family or the state but in the source of life, the Father; to the extent to which he can merge his life with that of the Father.[25]

When reasonable consciousness has indicated the deceptiveness of personal good, there is only one path left open to man, and that is the path of (spiritual) love, which provides its own real, inalienable good that is always within reach here and now.[26] The only reasonable relation a man can have to the world, therefore, consists in service of the source of life, which means that the animal personality should be subjected to reasonable consciousness; for reasonable consciousness, besides being that reason or spirit of negation that poisons personal life, is apparently God: it is proclaimed in Chapter x of *On Life* as the Logos of St John; and it appears to be the Reason of the Platonists and of Coleridge, and Kant's moral law.

The harmful effect that this dualism is likely to have can be seen in *The Kreutzer Sonata*, which shows the worst side of Tolstoy, with its furious insulting of the physical elements in human love. (The story is not written with sufficient detachment for one to be able to feel that the insults are artistically placed as a product of Pozdnyshev's derangement, and that they are not Tolstoy's own to an inordinate degree.) One cannot forget, when reading Tolstoy's religious essays, that his is a philosophy which has been born from despair. His earlier novels and stories often express a very vivid awareness of the beauty and richness of sensuous, physical life; and yet it was this life that he was going to destroy in himself, if the questioning of his reason could not be answered, if his spiritual yearning could not be satisfied. And when the answer was found, it proved to be one in view of which he saw meaning in the life of the body only in its function as an instrument of the spirit.

---

[25] *The Kingdom of God is Within You*, iv—where "*istochnik*" ("source") is used apparently synonymously with "*nachalo*", which may be translated as "principle", "beginning", "source", or "origin". See Chapter iii, section 6.

[26] *On Life*, xxii.

And from this belief in the complete subordination of the physical to the spiritual, there follow with apparent logic both the sex teaching—that celibacy is higher and worthier than matrimony—and the ideal of non-resistance to evil—the belief that no physical force should ever be used to defend the life of the body.

3 Inevitability, Freedom, and Non-Resistance

Now Tolstoy's ideal of non-resistance, which is based on the understanding that one should act according to principle, regardless of the consequences, is connected with the question of freedom and inevitability. When he wrote *What I Believe* (*V chëm moya vera?*) in 1883, probably being aware of the obscure wording of parts of the Epilogue, Part II, of *War and Peace*, he proclaimed:

> Free-will is not merely an illusion, it is a phrase devoid of meaning. It is a phrase invented by the theologians and criminalists, and to refute that phrase is to tilt at windmills; but reason—that which illumines our life and obliges us to alter our actions—is not an illusion and cannot be denied.[27]

He took up the problem again ten years later in *The Kingdom of God is Within You.*

We must "alter our actions"; like Christian, we must abandon the City of Destruction, renouncing this ruinous personal life. War, which in the great novel was shown to be ghastly but inevitable, is rejected utterly by the true Christian conscience. There is a terrible contradiction between our consciousness and our way of life. Our social system was founded on the belief that men could avoid the wretchedness of purely selfish lives, and the cruelty of the struggle between individuals, by replacing the attainment of personal, with the attainment of social, well-being as the aim of life. But not only is such a belief in itself quite pagan; our social system has manifestly failed to preserve us from misery and conflict. The supreme exposure of the betrayal is compulsory military service, by which working people in a country are made to oppress one another (did not the German Chancellor say that reliable

[27] *What I Believe*, VII.

NCOs were needed for the struggle against socialism?), are torn from their customary occupations, taxed for war preparations, held under a perpetual threat of war with other lands, and, worst of all, obliged to be the accomplices of their government in all its appalling crimes.[28] To end this evil, we must live henceforth according to the demands of our Christian consciousness: we must cease to acknowledge governments, must renounce the State and all its works, and give up all idea of defending ourselves by force, as to inflict violence is in itself wicked, and personal and social well-being are mere illusions.

But to form the decision to make this change in our lives, we need a degree of freedom. People who want to go on living as before will say:

> A man cannot change his life because he is not free, and he is not free because all his actions are conditioned by preceding causes. And whatever a man may do there are always such and such causes which oblige him to do such and such actions.

How shall we refute this opinion?

Tolstoy argues that man's freedom lies in the activity of reason—that is, in the choice between recognition and non-recognition of certain "truths" (*"priznanie istiny"*).

> Man would not be free if he knew no truth at all, and he would not be free or even have any idea of freedom, if the whole truth that should guide him in life were revealed to him once for all in complete purity with no admixture of error.

Some truths we were taught in childhood and never question; others we never consider because they are too distant from us. But there are truths of a third kind, which do not form the unconscious motives of action, and yet which affect us so closely that we cannot pass them by; "and it is in regard to these truths that man's freedom is manifest".[29]

As was said in *War and Peace*, we are free in our consciousness; but it was also said there that our actions are necessarily conditioned by time and place and subject to causation, so that in the performance of actions we are not free. Now, when

---

[28] *The Kingdom of God is Within You*, vii.
[29] *Ibid.*, xii, Conclusion, 5.

Tolstoy considers the activity of consciousness in *The Kingdom of God is Within You*, he claims that the recognition or non-recognition of a certain truth depends not on "external" causes but on some cause within the man himself, not subject to observation. Human life has an inner and an outer domain; the latter is a process that operates in time and space and by cause and effect, and the good of the animal personality depends upon it. A Christian, however, "cannot understand human life otherwise than as the submission of an animal personality to the law of reason"; and "this life, though manifested in time and space, is not determined by conditions of time and space, but only by the degree of the subjection of the animal personality to reason."[30] This degree of subjection is the cause within a man on which it depends whether he recognises a certain truth or not. As for what determines the degree of subjection to reason, one factor, among others, must be nothing less than an uncaused cause. Tolstoy quotes Christ: "No man can come to me, except the Father . . . draw him." What causes *"metanoia"*? Whatever the circumstances may be, sincere and deep *"metanoia"* is not possible without the agency of the divine element in man, reasonable consciousness or the self, which is free and has no antecedent cause.

A Christian will try not to perform any actions except in accordance with his inner recognition of truth. Realising that it would only ever be necessary to take up arms if the good of human life lay in the animal personality, he will refuse military service; and this refusal will result from his inner freedom. One of the mottoes of *The Kingdom of God is Within You* is: "Ye shall know the truth, and the truth shall make you free". Thus it is argued that there can be no question of liberating Christians or of depriving them of freedom, for Christians are free by definition.[31]

The argument disregards the psychological factors that help to determine what decision a man makes on an issue, apart from those factors relevant to the theory of dualism; and it overlooks the processes of reasoning that may be involved: it overlooks not only the questions of the nature of one's mental equipment and perception, and of the nature of what is

[30] *On Life*, xiv.   [31] *The Kingdom of God is Within You*, ix.

perceived, but even the processes of thinking and logic. But in this imaginary capacity to "recognise truth" independently of any cause, except for the degree of the submission of the animal personality to reason, is expressed, according to the essay *Believe Yourselves*, the "divine principle" (*"bozhestvennoe nachalo"*) that lives in each of us, and the awakening of which forms the theme of Tolstoy's address to adolescent boys and girls. The boys and girls are counselled to believe themselves only when the answers they give to life's questions are based, not on their personal desires, but on the desire to fulfil the will of that Power which sent them into life. The problem of the origin of these desires is not discussed. Why should the desire to do God's will not arise from the personality like other desires, and be fraught with deception? The awakening of the divine principle is associated with the beginning of the years of discretion, in contrast to a child's submission to the views of others.

To return to *War and Peace*: it was said there that in his "elemental swarm-life" man inevitably obeys laws laid down for him, and that the individual will is impotent in face of the course of history. This thesis, exaggerated as it is, was to have serious consequences; without being the cause of the subsequent ideal of non-resistance to evil, it gave it some of its apparently logical justification. For it seemed to Tolstoy that those human actions which are conditioned by the desire for personal well-being form a cohesive system, the nature of which is incomprehensible to us. The swarm-life is so complicated, and the causes affecting the conduct of each individual are so numerous, that we can never understand the course of history, even though it be predetermined. In *What I Believe*, which is the first work in which the ideal of non-resistance is announced, Tolstoy writes:

> People bound together by a delusion form, as it were, a collective cohesive mass. The cohesion of that mass is the world's evil. All the reasonable activity of humanity is directed towards the destruction of this cohesion.[32]

Attempts by revolutionaries to break up that mass by violence only forge it closer. Their activities afford an excuse for

[32] *What I Believe*, XII.

governments to intensify their power and become more despotic; and if they should succeed in seizing power, they would have themselves to become even more despotic than the government they overthrew.[33] There is only one way: "The force freeing each particle of the human cohesive mass is truth", for only truth, reasonable consciousness, the real and actual self, are beyond the conditions of the cohesive mass, and "man can hand on the truth only by deeds of truth".

In some places in *The Kingdom of God is Within You* Tolstoy professes to have insight into the course of history. He declares in Chapter x that, apart from the question whether the abolition of the State is desirable, men will outgrow the State as certainly as a chick breaks out from its shell when unable any longer to find enough room within it. But it is not minute examination of the chain of cause and effect that has enabled him to make this optimistic prediction. Further on, after expression of the theory that man's freedom lies in the choice between recognition and non-recognition of certain truths, he writes:

> His freedom does not consist in being able to act spontaneously, independently of the course of life and of the influence of existing causes, but it means that by recognizing and professing the truth revealed to him he can become a free and joyful participant in the eternal and infinite work performed by God or by the life of the world; or he can, by not recognizing that truth, become its slave and be painfully forced to go where he does not wish to go.

That chain of cause and effect discussed in *War and Peace*, by which one inevitable event was linked to another, appeared to be unbreakable because it seemed inconceivable that men should direct their energy towards any other goal than the good of themselves or of the group to which they belong. Consciousness, which is beyond the motion of history, though manifest in and animating it, could not break that chain of cause and effect or alter the course of events; but now it can, for the divine element in man reveals that the pursuit of personal or of social well-being is irrational. If consciousness is

[33] *The Kingdom of God is Within You*, VIII.

disregarded or taken as only a constant vital force, we know that the motion of history leads inevitably to war; but if reasonable consciousness, itself uncaused, is one of the factors that determine that the animal personality shall be subjected to reason to the extent of one's being convinced that personal or social well-being is illusory, then there is a breaking-in on the chain of cause and effect; we are free to recognise war as wrong, whatever the circumstances, and not to wage another. There is undue optimism, however, in the step Tolstoy stealthily takes from the proposition that men are free to repudiate the State and the practice of war, to the proposition that generally this repudiation will be made so frequently that mankind as a whole will outgrow the State. He can announce that it is a law of life that the welfare of an individual's personality is either freely renounced or, later, destroyed inevitably;[34] that is obvious; but he has little evidence for suggesting that voluntary renunciation is becoming more and more general, for saying:

> The forward movement of humanity . . . proceeds first and foremost because men in general are steadily and unceasingly advancing towards a more and more conscious assimilation of the Christian conception of life; and secondly because, even apart from any conscious spiritual activity, men are unconsciously brought to a more Christian attitude to life . . .[35]

He can point to a few examples and make remarks about the improvement of public opinion in modern Europe, but his inference is mere wishful thinking; we have only to use his own method—to take into consideration a larger or a smaller area, and a longer or a shorter period of time, than those which he arbitrarily selects—in order to refute it with ease. Therefore he has no grounds for speaking of "the eternal and infinite work performed by God or by the life of the world". The laws of cause and effect will continue to operate, with occasional breakings-in from reasonable consciousness as people are converted; we may see a divine influence in several places cutting into the chain of events which we previously contemplated.

---

[34] *On Life*, XVI.
[35] *The Kingdom of God is Within You*, X.

But the chain of events cannot be continuously fused with the divine influence: events that are offensive to conscience will probably always occur.

The recommendations made in *The Kingdom of God is Within You* are negative: Do not support the State or resist evil by force. Given Tolstoy's premises, what positive ones can we make? If personal and social well-being are delusions, there is no need to promote good government or resist evil. Whether they are or not, one has to submit to the conditions of the collective cohesive mass if one aims at furthering the good of society. Whoever attempted so to take part in politics as to act in accordance with his inner recognition of truth, would nevertheless find that he was obliged to make various compromises, to promise allegiance to someone, accept the authority of a superior or bow to the will of a majority, and that the nature of his actions was being determined more by the conditions of the cohesive mass than by his own consciousness. By the light of reason and truth he would desire one thing; but time, place, and causation would produce another. The inner consciousness is aware of demands which transcend anything that can be fulfilled by the laws of history, which are the laws of cause and effect. Persuade a man that it is wrong to resist evil, and he will dissociate himself from that terrible cohesion. His refusal to support either the government or the revolutionaries will be striking, and supposedly not explicable except as prompted by a divine power. He will bear witness to the need to act in exclusive and unconditional obedience to the law of reason. Then others—it is to be hoped—stirred by his example, will follow him, and the enchanted circle of social life will be destroyed, as, when one bee spreads its wings and flies from the cluster of bees that hangs from a branch, a second, a third and a hundredth will then do the same.[36] But persuade him to devote himself to society, and he will be surrounded by people making the same avowal; he may be well-meaning, but his actions will not manifest a power strong enough to transform human life. The cohesion of the mass will remain as firm as before; one bee will still cling to another.

[36] *Ibid.*, IX.

II

Death and Illumination

On 20th September he died, literally in my arms.... It is true, as he said, that nothing is worse than death. And when one reflects well that *that* is the end of all, then there is nothing worse than life. Why strive or try, since of what was Nicholas Tolstoy nothing remains his? . . . Some moments before his death he drowsed off, but awoke suddenly and whispered with horror: 'What is that?' That was when he saw it—the absorption of himself into Nothingness. And if he found nothing to cling to, what can I find? Still less!... A letter from Leo Tolstoy to A. A. Fet, 17 October 1860.[1]

1 Introduction

IN *War and Peace* and *Anna Karenina*, lying behind the detailed tracing of the flow of events in history and society is an inner movement towards illumination. These two novels contain gradually deepening processes of understanding, which reach their fulfilment, or the point as near to fulfilment as Tolstoy can bring them, in the contemplation of death. Pierre, Andrew, and Levin set out with their creator on heroic quests. But they hardly know what they are looking for, and the moments of illumination that are finally granted them, though seeming at the time to answer everything, prove, on examination, to have ambiguous messages. In *The Hedgehog and the Fox* [2] Sir Isaiah Berlin discusses these revelations and raises the question how far these in *War and Peace* and *Anna Karenina* differ from the teaching about the meaning of life that Tolstoy developed in his final, religious phase. "What is it that Pierre, Prince Andrey, Levin discover?" asks Sir Isaiah Berlin. What does Ivan Ilych discover? The story of his death was told after *What I Believe* had been completed; and Aylmer Maude can

---

[1] Quoted by Aylmer Maude in *The Life of Tolstoy*, Vol. I, Ch. VI, pp. 214-15.
[2] Ch. VI, pp. 99-108.

say [3] that the philosophic truth stated in *On Life* is presented in fictional form in *The Death of Ivan Ilych*. Yet not only are the theories expressed in Tolstoy's religious and metaphysical tracts highly questionable, but at their best they are general formulations the validity of which requires to be tested in the experience of individuals. Tolstoy, in his final attempts to harmonise his artistic and religious impulses, tried fiction and drama to demonstrate, not as a thesis but in terms of lived experience, the truth that he believed he had discovered, or to capture in art the truth that was for ever just eluding him.

"The relationship between thought and expression," says Dr Steiner,[4] "is at all times reciprocal and dynamic." The very intensity of Tolstoy's fiction may be due in part to his commitment to the belief that truth is discoverable. In *The Hedgehog and the Fox* Sir Isaiah Berlin says:

> Tolstoy's genius lies in a capacity for marvellously accurate reproduction of the irreproducible, the almost miraculous evocation of the full, untranslatable individuality of the individual, which induces in the reader an acute awareness of the presence of the object itself, and not of a mere description of it, employing for this purpose metaphors which fix the quality of a particular experience as such, and avoiding those general terms which relate it to similar instances by ignoring individual differences —'the oscillations of feeling'—in favour of what is common to them all.[5]

This is so; but perhaps what makes the objects and experiences so memorable is the metaphysical earnestness, the obsessive desire to come finally to terms with reality, to make something of it, to find its underlying principles while maintaining a sense of the diversity of its particulars. When Tolstoy maintained this tension between his perceptions and his beliefs, he achieved a characteristic double movement in his novels. There is the co-existence of, to use the words of Dostoevsky's devil, the most exalted manifestations of the human spirit and the last button on a shirt-front. Yet the inner and outer worlds in Tolstoy are not static; the spirit, struggling for illumination, is confronted

[3] In his preface to his translation of the story.
[4] *Tolstoy or Dostoevsky: An Essay in Contrast*, Ch. 4, i, p. 232.
[5] *The Hedgehog and the Fox*, III, p. 64.

with a baffling and ever shifting reality. Through his protagonists, he engages us in a progress towards truth related at every step to the experiences that he, as an artist, has necessarily reordered. The movement of events and the movement of the spirit are vitally interrelated. Yet it is the purpose of this chapter, with due caution, to study the latter, as it is developed in the protagonists, and to see what it is that Tolstoy presents as revelation.

Resurrection requires a separate examination. Nekhlyudov has something like a conversion early in the story,[6] and the novel has an inner movement peculiar to itself: it is not a search so much as a study of society in the light of discovered truth; deductions are made from that truth, and Nekhlyudov tries to live by it. Begun in 1895 and finished in 1899, *Resurrection* comes after all the works considered in this chapter, except *Hadji Murad*.

Pierre, Andrew, Levin, and Ivan Ilych, melancholic in their searches for meaning in life, stand in contrast to Uncle Eroshka, Natasha Rostova, Anna Karenina, and Hadji Murad, who, for all their inadequacies, seem to have that indefinable "spontaneous-creative fulness of being" which precludes the questions "What for?" and "Why?" [7] Anna's suicide through passion is contrasted with the metaphysical perplexity of Levin, who is "less horrified by death than by life without the least knowledge of whence it came, what it is for, why, and what it is".[8] Prince Andrew at times appears in abstraction from life; and Pierre at one period seems to be no more than "one of those retired gentlemen-in-waiting of whom there were hundreds, good-humouredly ending their days in Moscow":

---

[6] *Resurrection*, Part I, Ch. XXVIII.

[7] "To have achieved 'fulfilment' is to find meaning in life in the sense of having found immunity against the torments of the question, 'What for?', and found it, not by falling into inert day-to-dayness, the anaesthesia of habit or automatism, but by achieving what Lawrence elsewhere (and both the context of discourse in *Psychoanalysis and the Unconscious* and the art of *The Rainbow* and *Women in Love* make it very much more than a phrase) calls 'spontaneous-creative fulness of being'."— F. R. Leavis, *D. H. Lawrence: Novelist*. London (Chatto & Windus), 1955, p. 117. See "D. H. Lawrence and *Anna Karenina*", articles by Henry Gifford and Raymond Williams, in *Russian Literature and Modern English Fiction*, ed. Donald Davie.

[8] *Anna Karenina*, Part VIII, Ch. VIII.

"*Il est charmant; il n'a pas de sexe*", young ladies say of him.[9] Pierre and Levin reach metaphysical conclusions which to them serve as remedies, but which are stated in general terms as though true for all. Do they ask what the meaning of life is just because they are lacking in wholeness and oneness with life? Are their conclusions, therefore, a mere second-best, a kind of compensation, or are they indeed the gates to true life?

2 *Eroshka and Olenin*

The contrast between Olenin and Uncle Eroshka in *The Cossacks* is a case in point. The wealthy, cultured Moscovite, who has turned his back on his life in society, calling it "not the real thing", and who felt more and more light-hearted the nearer he drew to the Caucasus,[10] is impressed by the boisterous, sensual old Cossack.

Eroshka, massive and powerful, with a snow-white beard, and smelling of drink, gunpowder, and congealed blood, first appears like some pagan god of hunting, laden with equipment and game.[11] But although he rhapsodises on the joys of hunting, he dislikes killing: because the pig is God's creature, it is no worse than man and has its own inalienable law of being; and, when he has said so, Eroshka drives the moths away from the candle, so that they may not burn. Yet he is proud of his past, which consisted in plundering, killing, drinking, chasing women, and singing; he describes himself as "a wag" and promises to find a girl for Olenin: "God has made everything for the joy of man", he says.[12] A superannuated and solitary man, who, when drunk, weeps for his youth,[13] he is genuinely fond of Olenin and Lukashka, and has an immediate reverence for life.

Olenin vacillates. At one time he decides that happiness lies in self-sacrifice: "Since one wants nothing for oneself, why not live for others?"[14] But later he comes to see the self-deception in this attitude, and the wrongness of a self-renun-

[9] *War and Peace*, Vol. II, Part V, Ch. I.
[10] *The Cossacks*, Chs. II and III. *The Cossacks* was begun in 1852 and first published in 1863.
[11] *Ibid.*, Chs. VI and XI.   [12] *Ibid.*, Chs. XII and XIV-XVI.
[13] *Ibid.*, Ch. XXVIII.   [14] *Ibid.*, Ch. XX.

ciation that consists in doing good primarily to benefit oneself. At the same time, in recognising his love for Maryanka, he embraces a kind of nature-mysticism:

> I am not acting by my own will, but some elemental force loves through me; the whole of God's world, all nature, presses this love into my soul and says, "Love her". I love her not with my mind or my imagination, but with my whole being. Loving her I feel myself to be an integral part of all God's joyous world.

In contradistinction to a theory of self-renunciation very like that propounded in the essay *On Life*, which is based explicitly on dualism, Olenin now, perhaps having learnt from Eroshka, discovers a life-force that is no more to be denied in himself than it is in anyone or anything else. In this intuition of unity of being, however, the ethical question posed by his rivalry with Lukashka is rejected: "I do not now love those others . . ."[15]

Yet, of course, Olenin cannot become as one of the Cossacks. Not only can he not marry Maryanka, but he cannot attain the primitive immediacy and wholeness of Eroshka—as, indeed, is indicated by the awkwardness and seemingly second-hand quality of the phrases in which he expresses his nature-mysticism: "some elemental force", "God's joyous world", and so forth. Turgenev thought that the personality of Olenin spoilt the generally splendid impression of the book:

> To contrast civilization with fresh, primeval Nature there was no need again to produce that dull, unhealthy fellow always preoccupied with himself. Why does Tolstoy not get rid of that nightmare?[16]

At one time Olenin thought that his belief that happiness lies in self-sacrifice was preventing him from joining the Cossacks.[17] Are we intended to feel that this ascetic ideal results from his own weakness, from the moral disfigurement that was brought about by his past in Moscow? A sequel to the story was intended but never written. The nightmare, which could not

---

[15] *The Cossacks*, Ch. xxxiii.
[16] Quoted by Aylmer Maude in *The Life of Tolstoy*, Vol. i, Ch. ix, p. 295.
[17] *The Cossacks*, Ch. xxvi.

be got rid of, had to be lived through: Olenin's sickness is shared by Andrew, Pierre, and Levin.

3 Andrew and Pierre

In *War and Peace* (begun in 1863) in the persons of Pierre Bezukhov and Prince Andrew, the search for truth is carried on along two different paths. Pierre is always seeking for positive values, but lapses into despondency. He is seized with metaphysical despair after his separation from Hélène, and again, more seriously, after Natasha's engagement to Andrew and the death of Joseph Alexeevich.[18] He asks the big questions, "What is life, and what is death?" and wants to live for others, for his neighbour. He thinks at one time that in the creed of the Freemasons he has found an answer and a justification for philanthropic activity. Yet, besides being oppressed by the triviality and hypocrisy of the Masons, he finds that their beliefs do not solve the dreadful questions that concern him. To Andrew, on the ferry raft, he preaches God and a future life,[19] but this faith does not ease his perplexity for long.

> Whatever he tried to be, whatever he engaged in, the evil and falsehood of it repulsed him and blocked every path of activity. Yet he had to live . . .

His agony lies in facing life, from which all men seem to him to be seeking refuge. "Nothing is trivial, and nothing is important . . .", he thinks. "Only not to see *it*, that dreadful *it*!" All conventional values are abolished before the implacable destiny that appears repeatedly in Tolstoy under the pronoun "*it*".[20]

Andrew, active, stern, and gloomy, is tormented by a sense of the vanity of life and the unattainability of happiness. Yet at Austerlitz he not only realises the insignificance of Napoleon and of the glory that he himself has desired more than anything else, but also, in contemplation of that "equitable and kindly

---

[18] *War and Peace*, Vol. II, Part II, Ch. I, and Part V, Ch. I.

[19] *Ibid.*, Vol. II, Part II, Ch. XII.

[20] Here and in *The Death of Ivan Ilych* the feminine pronoun is used; elsewhere the neuter '*ono*' occurs.

sky", he finds a new beauty in life; he comes to believe in "the greatness of something incomprehensible but all-import-ant" and he wants to live; yet "only the heavens promised peace".[21] After this, when Pierre visits him at Bogucharovo, he counters Pierre's idea of love and self-sacrifice with a bitter kind of quietism, saying he has resolved to live for himself merely avoiding illness and remorse;[22] and it becomes apparent, as the two are talking together on the raft, that it is above all the death of his wife—when he, as he says, was left facing the abyss into which she had vanished—that prevents him from sharing Pierre's optimism. Pierre is then an ardent Freemason, naïvely confident, and yet his words about God revive some-thing in Andrew so that at that meeting a new life begins for the latter.

The conclusion of this scene, however, after the close of the conversation, is wooden.

> Something that had long been slumbering, something that was best within him, suddenly awoke, joyful and youthful, in his soul . . .

What Dr George Steiner says with reference to the presentation of Andrew in the moment in which he falls at Austerlitz, applies equally to this paragraph: speaking of "Tolstoy's in-ability to convey genuine disorder, to commit his style to the portrayal of mental chaos", Dr Steiner says that, when Tolstoy approached an episode or condition of mind not susceptible to lucid account, he inclined to evasion or abstraction.[23] A positive value is being offered us here, but it is not realised, and the reader is left with a form of words or mere promise.

Andrew's alternations between despair and attachment in the next Part are achieved better. The oak, first seen "rigid, misshapen, and grim", and later "spreading out a canopy of sappy dark-green foliage", and standing "rapt and slightly trembling in the rays of the evening sun", not only, as an image, registers for the reader Andrew's changing feelings, but also, as an object, symbolises for Andrew a glad renewal of life and

---

[21] *War and Peace*, Vol. I, Part III, Ch. XIX.
[22] *Ibid.*, Vol. II, Part II, Ch. XI.
[23] *Tolstoy or Dostoevsky*, Ch. 4, iv, p. 274.

activity. After seeming to say that life is a fraud, the oak becomes an embodiment of the emotions which Andrew experiences after his meeting with Natasha and his overhearing her delighting in the moonlit night.[24] Natasha, "overflowing with life", brings a new world to Prince Andrew, where he can believe in the possibility of happiness;[25] but after her unfaithfulness he loses, together with this belief, the intuitions which he associated with the sky he saw at Austerlitz:

> It was as if that lofty infinite canopy of heaven that had once towered above him had suddenly turned into a low solid vault that weighed him down, in which all was clear, but nothing eternal or mysterious.[26]

He turns eagerly to practical, military affairs, for they are a refuge—while the spiritual sullenness, approaching despair, that is in him, precluding any sort of reconciliation with Natasha, is placed in contrast with the joy and tenderness that Pierre feels after telling Natasha of his devotion to her, and that the comet of 1812 seems to symbolise for him.[27] Pierre's conception of Natasha transports him to a realm of beauty and love, where the questions "What for?" and "Why?" seem to lose their importance.[28]

As the war in Russia develops, Prince Andrew grows more and more bitter. The burning of Smolensk, the loss of Bald Hills and his father's death, these events all intensify the gloom that descended round him when Natasha broke her faith. He does not want to be reminded of his past and yet rides to Bald Hills, during the retreat, "with a characteristic desire to foment his own grief". Only one incident for a moment relieves his depression: he sees there, by chance, two little girls taking some plums and running away in fright—an event, Tolstoy says, that makes him realise the existence of other human interests quite different from his own and just as legitimate.[29]

---

[24] *War and Peace*, Vol. ii, Part iii, Chs. i-iii.
[25] *Ibid.*, Vol. ii, Part iii, Ch. xix.
[26] *Ibid.*, Vol. iii, Part i, Ch. viii.
[27] *Ibid.*, Vol. ii, Part v, Ch. xxii.
[28] *Ibid.*, Vol. iii, Part i, Ch. xix.
[29] *Ibid.*, Vol. iii, Part ii, Ch. v.

D

When he first saw Natasha, she made a similar impression on him. Generally he is self-centred, engrossed in affairs of his regiment, yet possessed by his own disillusionment. On the eve of Borodino he perceives, in the possibility of his own death, that all life is no more than a series of magic-lantern pictures, which he saw previously by artificial light through a glass, but which now appear in the cold white light of day. All the things that previously tormented or delighted him, or that seemed most important—glory, love, and even patriotism—are now "false images" seen in all their crudity. The anguish is that *he* should no longer exist, though life itself will go on; the birches outside and the smoke of the camp-fires seem terrible and menacing.[30]

In this mood he is visited by Pierre. Swayed by the ludicrous idea that Napoleon is the beast foretold in the Apocalypse and that he, Bezukhov, is predestined to put an end to his power, and now making to Andrew the most naïve remarks about military tactics, Pierre seems futile enough, without the other's hostility and sarcasm. Andrew has been impressed by Kutuzov, because Kutuzov is a man who can see the inevitability of the course of events and, acknowledging that it is stronger than his own will, can renounce his personal wishes.[31] Now to Pierre, Andrew develops what is in fact the Tolstoyan view of war, tactics, and morale. The scene suggests what a long way Pierre has to travel before he can attain any real understanding of life, and at the same time it takes us to the crisis of the novel. Stripping war of its false chivalry so as to reveal its horror, and having scoffed at the pacifism of the Freemasons, Andrew says that now, in view of what he has learnt, it is hard for him to live: "I see that I have begun to understand too much."[32] Hating the French and confident of victory, he knows not only the horror of war, but also the impotence of the individual will in the face of the course of events.

When on the battlefield he sees a smoking shell spinning beside him, he feels a new love for life, and the next moment

---

[30] *War and Peace* Vol. III, Part II, Ch. XXIV.
[31] *Ibid.*, Vol. III, Part II, Ch. XVI.
[32] *Ibid.*, Vol. III, Part II, Ch. XXV.

he is struck down; there is something in life he does not understand. In the ambulance station his thoughts gradually clear. Being undressed by an orderly reminds him of early childhood and of his nurse; and a sudden blissful feeling prepares him for the recognition of his enemy, Anatole Kuragin, sobbing on another table. The disgusting, but piteous sight of naked, bleeding bodies, the bliss that is always associated in Tolstoy with early childhood, the suffering of Kuragin and the unexpected recollection of Natasha as she appeared to Andrew at the ball—all this makes possible the illumination that comes to him:

> Compassion, love of our brothers, for those who love us and for those who hate us, love of our enemies; yes, that love which God preached on earth and which Princess Mary taught me and I did not understand—that is what made me sorry to part with life, that is what remained for me had I lived. But now it is too late. I know it![33]

These thoughts are developed in the next Part, as Andrew is lying in a hut at Mytishchi. As a presentation of interior monologue, Chapter xxxii of Volume iii, Part iii, is one of the most successful in Tolstoy; meditations are confused with the sensations and fantasies of the sick man. The religious insight has already been attained, and Andrew is now merely reflecting on it intermittently. He decides that there is a happiness which lies beyond material forces and is of the soul alone, and that divine love, which cannot change and does not require an object, is the very essence of the soul. He only now appreciates Natasha's sufferings and remorse, and, when she comes in, he is able to forgive her.

Shortly before his death, however, a change takes place in Prince Andrew, but one which is consistent with his previous thoughts. His sister and Natasha are horrified by his alienation from them, and by his coldness and indifference towards all that concerns the living. The nearer he seems to draw to the eternal, the more aloof he becomes from everything earthly. Divine love, far from making him sorry to part with life, unfolds within him, Tolstoy explains, "as if freed from the bondage of

---

[33] *Ibid.*, Vol. iii, Part ii, Chs. xxxvi and xxxvii.

life that had restrained it". As he grows in eternal love, he renounces life and overcomes the fear of death. Love for Natasha has been binding him to life and suppressing the feeling he had when he saw Kuragin at the ambulance station; but this human love—love with a particular object—disappears when the fear of death is finally vanquished.[34]

The analysis of Andrew's spiritual state during his last days relies considerably on the use of abstract, general terms; but his effect on Natasha and Princess Mary is vividly described, as are the impressions he has of Natasha when she is knitting by his side and also his dream of death. His thought that love is life and is God appears brain-spun to him, and is obscure, especially when compared with the vision of death that comes after it. He dreams that he is trying to hurry to lock the door, but his legs will not move, and he is frightened because "*it*" is behind the door. He cannot hold back the door; and "*it* entered, and it was *death*, and Prince Andrew died". But the same instant he wakes up, feeling as if powers within him have been liberated, but also, now, finally estranged from Natasha.

To overcome the fear of death is for Andrew to submit to death and be alienated from others; death is a victor with the gift of eternity. Pierre, too, burdened by freedom, tries to learn submission but learns it from others. "*They*", the soldiers at Borodino, the simple and sincere, are what he wants to become—or what he imagines the dead Joseph Alexeevich to be advising him to become; obedient to his benefactor, he must find the way of submission to God's will—endurance of war and acceptance of suffering. But his thoughts lack coherence.[35]

He has yet to discover the powerlessness of the individual will in the face of history. He thinks that the misery of Europe is solely due to Napoleon, wants to suffer, and is filled with contempt for everything men most value.[36] After his arrest, however, when he believes he has been sentenced to death, he discovers the truth that Andrew and Kutuzov are aware of,

---

[34] *War and Peace*, Vol. IV, Part I, Chs. XV and XVI.
[35] *Ibid.*, Vol. III, Part III, Ch. IX.
[36] *Ibid.*, Vol. III, Part III, Ch. XXVII.

but that is presented to him as a terrible contradiction of life, to which one cannot be reconciled: he is being killed, but by no one; no one but a system, a concurrence of circumstances, is annihilating him. At the execution of prisoners all the French are dismayed, not wanting to commit the murders they commit. Pierre's moral collapse is complete: "his faith in the right ordering of the universe, in humanity, in his own soul and in God, had been destroyed".[37] The contradiction consists in the fact that belief in the responsibility of individuals—oneself or Napoleon—is illusory, that events occur because they have to, and that these events, in which men are instrumental, crush humanity. During the retreat from Moscow, Pierre sees *"it"* again—the mysterious, callous, deterministic force that compels men to kill one another against their will; *"it"* is on the faces of the French and in their actions, so that Pierre is aware not of individuals but only of their movements.[38] Ready to learn submission, he is confronted by a brutal system to which men submit like automata.

This is the crisis of the novel; Pierre has reached the point Andrew reached when he said it was hard for him to live. In the executions Tolstoy presents in their harshest form those inexorable laws of history the reality of which he sets out to prove in the philosophic parts of the novel. *War and Peace* is evidently meant as a revelation of those laws and an attempt to find a basis for one's life when one is aware of them. And however shaky Tolstoy's theory of history may be on its positive side, however valid may be the distinction between determinism and fatalism, or however right Kareyev may be when he says that Tolstoy's notion of inexorable laws which work themselves out whatever men may think or wish is an oppressive myth, since, at least in the social sciences, laws are only statistical probabilities and not inexorable forces [39]—Pierre's experience at the executions is none the less real and his impression compelling: men commit crimes, when circumstances apparently require them, in such a way that no one seems to be personally to blame; in their collective lives they do things

---

[37] *Ibid.*, Vol. IV, Part I, Chs. X–XII.
[38] *Ibid.*, Vol. IV, Part II, Chs. XIII and XIV.
[39] Quoted by Sir Isaiah Berlin in *The Hedgehog and the Fox*, III, p. 55.

which each would not do if he regarded himself as responsible. Pierre finds himself in a world of senseless killing, but discovers a new foundation for his life almost immediately—in the person of Karataev.

The weakness of what follows has been pointed out quite convincingly by Dr Steiner:[40] the tendency towards abstraction and generality in the portrayal of Karataev, the rhetorical, external statements, Tolstoy's narrative omnipotence leading to didacticism; Karataev is described as "an unfathomable, rounded, eternal personification of the spirit of simplicity and truth".[41] Equally valid is Dr Steiner's criticism of Pierre's solipsism. Pierre comes to feel that the power of life in himself is independent of the fatal force that is crushing him. Not content to assert that power in revolt against the external force, he attempts to rise above the latter in contemplation, by holding that the whole magnificent night scene that he sees is himself and is in himself, so that it is ludicrous to suppose that "all that" night scene can be shut up in a shed,[42] or that he can be the victim of circumstances. "The idea which Pierre expounds runs counter to the general tone of the scene and to its intended lyric effect," says Dr Steiner.[43] More than that, it is an attempt to overcome the laws of history by denying the whole theory of them. If consciousness is all, then there is nothing outside us to crush us. This idea of consciousness differs from that put forward in the Epilogue, Part II, where consciousness is seen as but one of two sources of cognition, and is related to the other, reason, which expresses the laws of inevitability, as content is related to form.

After the executions the universe is meaningless to Pierre. Then he meets Karataev, and watches him deftly removing his legbands. What is impressive about Karataev, besides his kindness and his wisdom, is his pleasurable acceptance of small

---

[40] *Tolstoy or Dostoevsky*, Ch. 4, iv, p. 275.
[41] *War and Peace*, Vol. IV, Part I, Ch. XIII. R. F. Christian comments on the "bookish" nature of Karataev's peasant speech—"carefully culled on the evidence of Tolstoy's notes and drafts from Dal's *Proverbs of the Russian People* and retailed in an improbably concentrated form."—*Tolstoy's 'War and Peace': A Study*, Ch. I, p. 44.
[42] *War and Peace*, Vol. IV, Part II, Ch. XIV.
[43] *Tolstoy or Dostoevsky*, Ch. 4, iv, pp. 278-9.

things, his directness and spontaneity; he seems to be in immediate and affectionate contact with everything. Whereas Andrew finds on his deathbed that "all our feelings, all those ideas that seem so important to us, are *unnecessary*", "the commonest events . . . assumed in Karataev's speech a character of solemn fitness".[44] Andrew's spiritual conflict is resolved into antagonism between incompatibles, life and eternity; eternal love grows in him with a root of despair. Karataev is attached to everything as though he sees a world in a grain of sand and a heaven in a wild flower. Karataev, because of what he is—his wholeness, his roundness—sees the universe as a spiritual and physical whole; for Andrew the finite must be discarded before the infinite is attainable. Andrew resigns the life of the body; Pierre is bitterly deprived of the spirit; and, when Pierre recognises the spirituality of Karataev, he sees that it is in a vital and fruitful relation to earthly life. Suddenly in Karataev the possibility of complete harmony is suggested—a harmony consisting in a union of the individual consciousness with the world surrounding it—only for the two to be remorselessly torn apart in the apparently inescapable duality of life and divine love that is presented in the account of Andrew's death.

How indeed can Karataev maintain that unity of being in the face of death, of "*it*", the conscienceless movement of time and of history? His life, we are told, "had meaning only as part of a whole of which he was always conscious"; in his deep, intuitive wisdom he is at one, says Sir Isaiah Berlin, with the medium, the flow, the framework of life and its processes—that is to say, with the force that determines us and that results in war and death. The soldiers who shoot Karataev have on their faces an expression resembling what Pierre saw on the face of a young soldier at the executions.[45] To be at one with the force that crushes you is to be reconciled to death. Karataev, content to resign his body, is in consciousness a part of the whole; but that whole is the fatal force, the inexorable law of history that is recognised by reason and by virtue of which men have no freedom; and "a man having no freedom cannot

[44] *War and Peace*, Vol. IV, Part I, Chs. XIII and XV.
[45] *Ibid.*, Vol. IV, Part III, Ch. XIV.

be conceived of except as deprived of life".[46] But men do have a sense of personal responsibility, and it is precisely this that the French soldiers attempt to suppress in themselves when they obey orders and kill. Every time Pierre recognises in dismay the force of that fatal "*it*", his very dismay testifies that the inexorable laws of history are not the only reality, and announces a value affirmed by consciousness. If belief in personal responsibility is illusory, then the horror is illusory; but, as it is, the horrifying tension lasts as long as Pierre and Andrew are unable to come to terms with that overwhelming force. The moment Andrew resigns his life and his love for the gift of eternity, there is tranquillity and no tension; and again there would be tranquillity and no tension, if the French soldiers could indeed utterly forget the consciousness that dismays them and act like complete automata, and if Pierre could accept such a fact. Human nature and the reality of human responsibility are upheld not by the assertion of an eternal love that estranges one from earthly life, but by the fact that, however reconciled Karataev and Pierre may be to their own misfortunes, the soldiers that kill Karataev and others look guilty, and Pierre notices this.

Pierre benefits from his imprisonment, in that contemplation of death convinces him of the futility of the concerns which used to seem very important—that he was required to kill Napoleon, or that his wife was disgracing his name—and because in privation he undergoes the discipline which he needed all his life.

> The absence of suffering, the satisfaction of one's needs, and consequent freedom in the choice of one's occupation, that is, of one's way of life, now seemed to Pierre to be indubitably man's highest happiness,[47]

while "all unhappiness arises not from privation but from superfluity". Actually the only thing that causes Pierre real suffering is the state of his feet; the other discomforts provide a welcome discipline, so that it is hard to see how the context warrants the statement that "there is nothing in the world that is terrible"[48]—a statement which comes only a few pages after

---

[46] *War and Peace*, Epilogue, Part II, Ch. VIII.
[47] *Ibid.*, Vol. IV, Part II, Ch. XII.   [48] *Ibid.*, Vol. IV, Part III, Ch. XII.

the account of the death of Petya Rostov and just before that of Karataev's murder. Pierre is concerned now with his own position as a victim; Russia, the war, politics, and Napoleon are no business of his. He is enjoying a kind of limited, inner regeneration which reconciles him to his own misfortunes, but does not enable him to judge anything else.

When he hears Karataev's story of the merchant, he shares Karataev's joy—joy of "mystic significance". As a story of acknowledgment of guilt and of forgiveness, it is an assertion not only of man's personal responsibility, but also of a divine, redeeming freedom. "God will forgive you, we are all sinners in His sight".[49] This is the key to Pierre's salvation: he comes to believe in God. "Life is everything. Life is God," he hears in a dream, and this is explained by an image: everything that lives reflects God to the greatest possible extent.[50] Pierre no longer asks "What for?" or seeks for the aim of life, because he has faith in God. It is enough to live and have faith, for that is to feel free. He has learnt now what his nurse told him, that God is here and everywhere, for He is infinite and could be seen in Karataev as in everything. Pierre throws away the mental telescope through which, in his search for God, he gazed over men's heads, and gladly contemplates the infinite life around him.[51]

His newly found religion is an extension of the affirmation of life that is made in Karataev: God is immanent, and the truth is at our feet. Pierre's final insights are therefore in contrast with Prince Andrew's, just as previously, at Bogucharovo, Pierre's positive attitudes were contrasted with Andrew's negative ones. The more closely Pierre regards the infinite, the happier he becomes, and nothing, apparently, needs to be renounced.

His experience gives him a kind of stability, tranquillity and freshness, so that he appears to have just come out of a moral bath.[52] The fruits of his faith are to be seen in the transformation of his character; and, as Sir Isaiah Berlin says, when

[49] *Ibid.*, Vol. IV, Part III, Ch. XIII.
[50] *Ibid.*, Vol. IV, Part III, Ch. XV.
[51] *Ibid.*, Vol. IV, Part IV, Ch. XII.
[52] *Ibid.*, Vol. IV, Part IV, Ch. XVII.

he and Natasha, and Nicholas and Princess Mary are anchored in their sober, new lives at the end of the novel, they have all evidently achieved a kind of peace, based on some degree of understanding of the need to submit to the permanent relationships of things and the universal texture of human life, wherein alone truth and justice are to be found.

It is hardly out of accord with his faith when Pierre, realising how he loves Natasha, feels that his freedom has completely gone, or when, in his joyful frenzy, he sees the whole meaning of life centred in his love and the possibility of being loved by her.[53] In the Epilogue, Part I, Chapter x, we are given the Tolstoyan ethics of marriage, together with a dismal account of Pierre's subjection to his wife: he accepts her view that every moment of his life belongs to her and to the family, while in other ways Natasha is his slave. Absorbed in their marriage, they live contented but limited lives, when to live life fully and soberly is held to be the highest wisdom. No distinction is made here between the demands of the spirit and those of the personality; the need only is for tranquillity and fulness and unity of being. Faith in God in the novel seems to mean confidence in life as Karataev understands it; and Karataev, as Pierre says, would have approved of his and Natasha's family life,[54] in spite of what Dr Steiner with good reason calls its "tyrannical domesticity".[55]

He would not, however, as Pierre admits at the same time, have approved of the society which Pierre forms in the hope that honest men will join hands for the public welfare. The object of this society is to prevent some catastrophic rebellion by counteracting the most reactionary tendencies of the government. Pierre's idea of "active virtue" by "honest folk" is rather naïve and hardly thought out, and it takes no account of the message of the book about the forces that control history. R. F. Christian rightly complains that, the digressive, philosophic passages being concerned mainly with the big groups— whether nations or armies—the individual heroes are, as individuals, given only the scantiest treatment in the digressions

---

[53] *War and Peace*, Vol. IV, Part IV, Chs. XVI and XIX.
[54] *Ibid.*, Epilogue, Part I. Ch. XVI.
[55] *Tolstoy or Dostoevsky*, Ch. 2, vi p. 109.

and have the small area of freedom ascribed to them inadequately defined.[56] Pierre's formation of a society is perhaps no more than a sign of good intentions. Indeed the philosophic parts are not artistically integrated with the work as a whole, so that, in Dr Christian's words, Tolstoy's conclusions, while they can in retrospect be applied to the behaviour of the fictitious characters and can be made to seem not inconsistent with this behaviour, do not strike the reader spontaneously as he reads the stories of the Rostovs and the Bolkonskis, and the consistency between the idea and the fictional illustration of the idea has to be looked for. A good novel is one in which the artist has succeeded in expressing a quality perceived in life that cannot be reduced to a simple formulation, and that is conveyed by the work as a whole; it contains an objective world that lies between the author and his readers, and by virtue of which—by selection and dramatisation of the material—the author's insights, ideas, and feelings (which are what he essentially wishes to communicate, in the living stress of the novel) can carry conviction. *War and Peace* suffers from a certain disparity between the search for a unified vision of the world that Tolstoy carries on in his elaboration of a theory of history, and the search for God that Pierre undertakes. Tolstoy's quest ends in a form of necessitarianism, the bleakness of which is relieved only by a theory of consciousness that grants man internal freedom—that is to say, he arrives at a form of metaphysical dualism. But what Andrew and Pierre discover cannot be simply formulated; theirs are experiences, however, that do culminate in distinct beliefs—in divine love and in God. The insight that Andrew finally attains is a development of Tolstoy's metaphysical dualism; only it is an insight you can die with but not live with: Andrew renounces the life in which, anyway, it is impossible to *act* in freedom and according to conscience. Pierre's moral world collapses when he is dramatically confronted with "that dreadful *it*" at the executions, but he is able to reorient his life according to the insights he receives from his association with Karataev. What is wrong here is not only the slight air of unreality that there is about Karataev, but also the incompatibility of Pierre's idea

[56] *Tolstoy's 'War and Peace'*, Ch. IV, p. 146.

of God with the dualism of the Epilogue, Part II. Actually
Volume IV, Part IV, Chapter XII, which sets out Pierre's new
belief, is so vague that it says very little; but the idea of God
that is announced here cannot be equated with the conception
of consciousness as limited that is advanced at the end of the
novel. All the Epilogue, Part II, would allow one to say is that
Pierre finds an *inner* freedom that is not illusory. His discovery
of God appears to solve everything, but only appears to.
Whereas Pierre learns to see the infinite in everything and finds
tranquillity, Tolstoy arrives at a theory whereby war is held to
be inevitable and conscience sterile. The aim in each case is
to find a unifying principle underlying the diversity of experience; but hard-headed theorising produces one conclusion,
and intuition another. What is Pierre to do? There is no
escape from "*it*" except in death. He recognises his past folly
and accepts new responsibilities; family life is presented to
him and to the reader as an indubitable good. However, this
is not to resolve the tragic issue of the novel, but only to say
that, even after the most tragic experiences, life must go on,
and that suffering may purify. Pierre gradually comes to feel
in his being the deeper rhythms of life, and approaches the
state of Karataev. This is conveyed to the reader, with a certain lack of assurance, in fictional form. But the intellectual
problem remains: those deeper rhythms, the flow and framework of life, have (supposedly) been proved to be iron laws
leading to slaughter and death.

4 "*The Arzamas Misery*"

This is the name that Tolstoy gave to an event which
happened to him in September 1869, very soon after he had
finished writing *War and Peace*. He mentioned it briefly in a
letter on 4 September, calling it "such a dreary sensation . . .
as I had never felt before". His son Sergei suggests that it was
perhaps due to a liver complaint or to mental exhaustion, and
he records a similar event that occurred in 1875; but he also
understood that the fear of death was very closely associated
with it.[57] Years later, in 1884, Tolstoy wrote a fragment called

---

[57] *Tolstoy Remembered by his Son*, Sergei Tolstoy, translated by Moura Budberg,
pp. 10, 25-6, 171.

The Memoirs of a Madman, in which he described "the Arzamas misery" in fictional form.[58]

He was going to Penza to buy an estate, continued to travel by night and awoke suddenly filled with dread of death. He put up at a hotel in Arzamas, and was shown into a small, square room with white-washed walls and a red curtain. There he fell asleep, and awoke in torment:

> 'Why and whither am I escaping? I am running away from something dreadful and cannot escape it. I am always with myself, and it is I who am my tormentor . . . . I want to fall asleep and forget myself and cannot. I cannot get away from myself!'
>
> . . . I had gone out into the corridor thinking to escape from what tormented me. But *it* had come out with me and cast a gloom over everything. . . .
>
> 'What am I afraid of?'
>
> 'Me!' answered the voice of Death, inaudibly. 'I am here!'

Death is, and ought not to be; the glow of the candle and everything else round him repeated the same horror:

> 'There is nothing in life. Death is the only real thing, and death ought not to exist.'
>
> . . . Everything was hidden by the terrible consciousness that my life was ebbing away. . . . Life and death somehow merged into one another. Something was tearing my soul apart and could not complete the severance. . . . Always the same horror: red, white, and square. . . .

What he felt was a kind of spiritual nausea, a dull spitefulness towards himself and whatever or whoever had created him. He began to pray, but that was useless; and only after driving off did he feel better, though he knew that the depression could not be forgotten and felt that it had poisoned his life.

He tried to live without stopping to think what the misery might mean, and to live as before. But this he could not do. *The Memoirs of a Madman* record another attack, which took

[58] Aylmer Maude prefaces his translation with the remark: "As was usual with him when writing fiction, he drew on his personal experiences and even used the names of places and incidents that are mentioned in his diaries and correspondence."

place in a small hotel bedroom in Moscow—where the symptoms, the horror and the questioning, were similar. And a third occurrence is described, when the "madman" lost his way when hunting in a forest deep in snow—but this time some sort of joy resulted, as if after a conversion.

There is a striking similarity between the symptoms of the dying Ivan Ilych and an image that Tolstoy uses in his *Confession*[59] to describe the onset of what he calls these "moments of perplexity and arrest of life", which, during the 1870's, recurred more and more often:

> Then occurred what happens to everyone sickening with a mortal internal disease. At first trivial signs of indisposition appear to which the sick man pays no attention; then these signs reappear more and more often and merge into one uninterrupted period of suffering. The suffering increases and, before the sick man can look round, what he took for a mere indisposition has already become more important to him than anything else in the world—it is death!

Whether or not "the Arzamas misery" was due to a liver complaint does not matter. In the 1870's, when he had more than thirty years of life in front of him, Tolstoy realised vividly that he would have to die, and that the process of decay was already beginning; only he realised this with pathological intensity, as if, like Ivan Ilych, he had already contracted a fatal disease. He quickly felt that the chief horror consisted not in death but in the fact that one had to live when death was to follow. It was this that made life appear a stupid and spiteful joke someone had played on him, and that drew him towards suicide.[60] The Death that haunts the "madman" is the same "*it*" as the "*it*" of *War and Peace*: it is the physical process to which we owe our bodily life, that carries us along with it, and that will finally destroy us. The death of which Prince Andrew dreamt, and the callous force that dismayed Pierre, the system of events that controls us, suddenly became to Tolstoy a dreadful presence directly affecting himself; and his protest against death became a protest against the whole kingdom over which death reigns. A day or two before the original occurrence of "the Arzamas misery", on 30

[59] *Confession*, III.   [60] *Ibid.*, IV.

August 1869, Tolstoy wrote to Fet saying that he had been having an unceasing ecstasy over Schopenhauer, and that he was confident that Schopenhauer was the greatest genius among men.[61] Making a strange reversal of his thoughts at Arzamas, he believed for a time in the correctness of Schopenhauer's conclusions, which he summed up as follows: "Life is that which should not be—an evil; and the passage into Nothingness is the only good in life." [62] Similarly Andrew at first tried to lock death out, but then died gladly.

5 Levin

While writing *Anna Karenina* (from 1873 to 1877), Tolstoy endured his worst depression and came near to committing suicide. He says in his *Confession*[63] that he devoted himself to authorship as a means of stifling within himself all questions as to the meaning of his own life or life in general. Yet his moral, if not his metaphysical, preoccupations predominate in *Anna Karenina* as in *War and Peace*. Writing came to him inevitably as a part of living, and hence as an assertion of life, so that in the 1870's he was torn between assertion and denial. At the same time the need to find an answer to the question what life meant was urgent, because without an answer he felt he could not live, so that in seeking for an answer he was acknowledging his will to live.

Distinctions are made in *Anna Karenina* between artificial life and real life, and between apparently spontaneous actions and those resulting from a sense of duty or propriety. The former distinction is made explicitly when Karenin reflects for the first time on the possibility of his wife's unfaithfulness, and in that contemplation is like a man who, while crossing a bridge, suddenly sees that it is collapsing and that he is facing the abyss beneath. "The abyss was real life; the bridge was the artificial life Karenin had been living." [64] Until then he was in refuge from life, as at one time all men seemed to be to Pierre Bezukhov. Again, it appears to be something entirely new that enters his life when, kneeling beside the sick Anna, he

---

[61] Quoted by Aylmer Maude in *The Life of Tolstoy*, Vol. I, Ch. IX, p. 311.
[62] *Confession*, VI.   [63] *Ibid.*, III.
[64] *Anna Karenina*, Part II, Ch. VIII.

finds that he can gladly forgive her and Vronsky. He then resembles Prince Andrew, when the latter lay in the ambulance station on a table near his enemy Kuragin. Karenin's perturbation at the sight of other people's suffering becomes a state of bliss:

> He was not thinking that the law of Christ, which all his life he had wished to fulfil, told him to forgive and love his enemies, but a joyous feeling of forgiveness and love for his enemies filled his soul.[65]

But the feeling does not endure under the influence of society, when Anna recovers and renews her adultery. The tragic chain of circumstance, though broken once, is restored, and disaster becomes inevitable.

The love of Anna and Vronsky appears as an irruption of deep and real passion in a society of pettiness and false values. It is both immoral, in that it is against the standards of that society, and inherently tragic. But it cannot be judged unless it is seen in contrast with Constantine Levin's search for truth and his attempt to live a harmonious and sober life in the country. Permanent and acceptable values are sought in the rhythms of country life, in the traditional wisdom of the peasants, and in the establishing by man of a relation between himself and the universe of a sort that cannot exist for the town-dweller.

> In *Anna Karenina* [says Dr Steiner] the contrast between the city and the land is, quite obviously, the axis around which the moral and technical structure of the novel revolves. The whole of Levin's salvation is prefigured in his arrival in the country after the unsuccessful proposal to Kitty.[66]

Levin, a "seeker", full of doubts and dissatisfaction with himself, but a sincere and sympathetic man, is repelled by the frivolity and artificiality of society, and by the intellectual self-assurance of such as his brother Koznyshev and Katavasov.[67] The contrast between Levin and Koznyshev at the begin-

---

[65] *Anna Karenina*, Part IV, Ch. XVII.
[66] *Tolstoy or Dostoevsky*, Ch. 2, v, pp. 90-1.
[67] *Anna Karenina*, Part VIII, Ch. XVI.

ning of Part III is interesting, because it shows how much nearer Levin is to the peasants than Pierre Bezukhov could ever have been. It was part of Pierre's salvation that he should live his married life with Natasha in the country, but this idea is hardly developed; and, whereas he followed Karataev, the "natural man", out of the burning city rather as Dante followed Virgil (as Dr Steiner suggests), Levin lives and works among the peasants as their partner in a common undertaking:

> He could not like or dislike the people as if they were something apart, because he not only lived among them, his interests closely bound up with theirs, but he considered himself one of the people and could not find in himself any special qualities or defects which placed him in contrast with them.

A picture of Levin, his attitudes and problems, is given in the first four Parts of the novel, before the occurrence in Part V of the two decisive events in his life—his marriage, and the death of his brother Nicholas.

When Levin is arguing with Koznyshev, he is often guilty of self-contradiction, having no fixed views. The quietism which he opposes to his brother's concern for the general welfare resembles the attitude which Andrew maintained in dispute with Pierre at Bogucharovo—only without the bitterness: "I believe that in any case the motive power of all our actions is our personal happiness." [68] At the same time he is troubled by the question of marriage, which he usually regards as "the chief thing in life, on which the whole happiness of life depended",[69] but which is at present not possible for him. During his night on the haycock, however, oppressed by his loneliness and idleness, and envying the peasants their joyful, common toil, he decides to renounce his education and his dreams of a family life, and labour like a peasant. But this is not for long. On catching sight of Kitty—her complicated refinement being contrasted with the simplicity of the peasants—he realises that it is impossible, because of his love for her.[70] And although his attempts to introduce better agricultural methods are continually frustrated and give rise to hostility towards him among

[68] *Ibid.*, Part III, Ch. III.   [69] *Ibid.*, Part I, Ch. XXVII.
[70] *Ibid.*, Part III, Ch. XII.

E

the peasants, he maintains his hope, and is at times glad to think of his working for the public welfare.[71]

When in this state of mind, he is confronted with death: his sick brother Nicholas comes to see him. Levin is shocked by Nicholas's emaciation and his coughing, and is exasperated by the fact that they cannot be sincere with each other since neither will admit that Nicholas is dying. Levin remembers the pillow-fights that he and his brother used to have as children, which symbolise for him that spontaneity and joy of living in which it is impossible to think of death. But now the thought of death is utterly defeating: as it will come to him, too, and end everything, he feels that it is useless to begin anything and there is no help for it. Though strong and healthy, he says that he (Levin) is going to die soon, and that in face of death everything becomes insignificant. Yet he clings to his work, as it is all he has to cling to.[72]

This gloom disappears when he sees Kitty again and she accepts his proposal, and he is overcome by a delirious joy. Marriage brings quarrels and disappointments, but also "new and unexpected enchantments".[73] But, after only a few months of this new life, he hears that Nicholas is on his death-bed. Kitty insists on going with him, to nurse her dying brother-in-law, and astonishes Levin both by the efficiency of her nursing and by the strength of her conviction of the need for the dying man to receive Communion and Extreme Unction; evidently knowing just what is required in the face of death, she appears to Levin to know also with certainty what life and death are, whereas Levin, an agnostic, knows nothing and can do nothing.

Nicholas, also an unbeliever, takes Communion and Extreme Unction, partly out of an irrational hope of recovery and partly to please Kitty. Levin prays during the sacrament, but his prayer is conditional: "If Thou dost exist, heal this man . . . and Thou wilt save both him and me!" When it seems that Nicholas is really dying, Levin has the impression that something is becoming clear to the dying man which for himself remains as dark as ever, and Nicholas murmurs, "Yes, yes!

[71] *Anna Karenina*, Part III, Chs. XXIV and XXX.
[72] *Ibid.*, Part III, Chs. XXXI and XXXII, and Part IV, Ch. VII.
[73] *Ibid.*, Part V, Ch. XIV.

That's so!" as if discovering something. But Nicholas's illness and pain continue; irritable and demanding attention, he is possessed above all by the desire to be released from his pain and from its source—his body. Levin, who envies him his new knowledge, is plunged by his death into horror and perplexity; only Kitty's love saves him from despair, and that and her pregnancy give him ground again for living and loving.[74]

Boris Eykhenbaum thought that Nicholas Levin was modelled on both Nicholas and Dmitri Tolstoy, and that more was taken from the former than from the latter. This is not the usual view. Further, the description of Nicholas Levin's death, according to Aylmer Maude, was much more closely drawn from that of Dmitri than from that of Nicholas Tolstoy. But when Dmitri Tolstoy died in 1856, Leo was not very troubled,[75] whereas Nicholas's death in 1860 affected him as profoundly as Nicholas Levin's death affects his brother Constantine.

When Nicholas Tolstoy died, Leo was not married. By the deliberate juxtaposition of Nicholas Levin's death and the discovery of Kitty's pregnancy, Tolstoy creates a sense of the inevitable flow of life, and confronts his hero with two mysteries that are in essence one. After witnessing the death of his brother, and being accordingly inclined, but for Kitty, to deny life, Levin immediately finds himself overwhelmed by one infinite and mysterious process that is both horrifying and joyful. When, later, Kitty is about to give birth, he is reminded of what happened on his brother's death-bed; that sorrow and this joy both seem to him like openings in the usual conditions of life, through which something higher, beyond the reach of reason, becomes visible.[76] Nicholas Tolstoy's horrified "What is that?" appeared to mean that the dying discover nothing but the vanity of life, and perhaps Nicholas Levin's "Yes, yes! That's so!" indicates no more. But, whereas Nicholas Levin's death is described from the point of view of an onlooker, in the deaths of Prince Andrew, Ivan Ilych, and Vasili Andreevich

[74] *Ibid.*, Part v, Chs. xix and xx.

[75] B. M. Eykhenbaum, *Lev Tolstoy*, Book 1, *the 1850's*, Part 1, Ch. v, p. 122. Aylmer Maude's note to his translation of *Anna Karenina*, Part iii, Ch. xxxi. Maude's *Life of Tolstoy*, Vol. 1, Ch. v, p. 148.

[76] *Anna Karenina*, Part vii, Ch. xiv.

in *Master and Man,* Tolstoy attempts to trace the thoughts of
the dying man and to reveal that realm which is beyond the
reach of reason. In *Anna Karenina* it is not until Levin con-
verses with a peasant in Part VIII that an answer is given.

The death of his brother is the occurrence that provokes
Levin's metaphysical perplexity, just as Tolstoy's outlook on
life was fundamentally altered by Nicholas Tolstoy's death
and "the Arzamas misery". But, while Levin's search for
truth is a reflection of the search which Tolstoy was carrying
on in the 1870's, his plight never has the terrible and morbid
intensity of "the Arzamas misery", as the latter is described
in *The Memoirs of a Madman,* and the closing chapters of *Anna
Karenina* seem quite mild when compared with the *Confession,*
which, up to a point, tells the same story.

For Levin scientific notions have replaced the Christianity
in which he was brought up, but he is oppressed by the fact
that they supply no guidance and do not give life a meaning.
Rejecting the artificialities of the metaphysicians, Levin involuntarily accepts the current materialism, which has the
merit of clarity; but that he is no more than a bubble maintaining itself awhile in an infinity of time, space, and matter, is not
only "a distressing falsehood" but "the cruel mockery of some
evil power". It is impossible to submit to that power, but there
is a way to free oneself from it, which is by suicide.[77] First
death demonstrates the futility of our lives, and then it appears
we are to escape from that futility by embracing death. In
his *Confession* Tolstoy says that he regarded it as mere weakness
not to commit suicide when you have realised the meaning-
lessness of life.[78] But Levin does not follow Anna. One reason,
perhaps, is that, although suicide presents itself to her as a
means of escape, it is essentially acceptance of the futility of
man's fate, since death is part of the system that controls us.
Here is Pierre Bezukhov's plight again: if there was nothing
in life but a mechanical process, we should not have the power
to protest against that process. Karenin has already shown that
a tragedy could be reversed by endless forgiveness; now Levin
returns to those Christian values, which are based on something
other than the chain of cause and effect.

[77] *Anna Karenina,* Part VIII, Ch. IX. 　　　[78] *Confession,* VII.

In his *Confession* Tolstoy goes on to say, "I see now that if I did not kill myself it was due to some dim consciousness of the invalidity of my thoughts." Similarly, Levin is aware of the "falsehood" of the materialism that torments him. He has, as he discovers later, been living well but thinking badly, and is only able to live at all thanks to the beliefs in which he was brought up. The force of these beliefs in him has already been manifest in his tendency to pray at any moment of serious crisis; and in his dealings with the peasants he unhesitatingly follows the dictates of his conscience—that "infallible judge" within him. But the point is made that he cannot understand why he should pray, so that he is out of harmony with himself, being governed by a tradition that he cannot accept intellectually.[79]

Illumination comes to him in a brief exchange with a peasant, Theodore, who remarks that the innkeeper Mityuka only thinks about stuffing his belly, but that Plato, another peasant, is an upright old man, who lives for his soul and remembers God. Levin recognises in these words the essence of the Christian tradition, and he acknowledges that he has never doubted its truth, and neither has anyone else. This truth is beyond reason, and knowledge of it was not acquired but given, for when it was taught in childhood, he was told only what was already in his soul. Whereas reason teaches the law of the struggle for existence, the truth is that one must love one's neighbour and live for God and the soul, where the meaning of life resides. For goodness has no cause and no reward, so that it is beyond the chain of cause and effect. In this way what seemed to be a cruel, mocking power is replaced by a God to Whom one can joyfully submit; for, while to live for one's own needs is to acknowledge nothing but reason and a process that ends in death, to love one's neighbour is to get outside that process.[80]

These are, of course, the ideas that form the basis of Tolstoy's subsequent religious teaching, in which they are developed and clarified. In the novel it is not clear what is meant by loving one's neighbour rather than living for one's own needs,

[79] *Anna Karenina*, Part VII, Ch. XIII, and Part VIII, Chs. VIII, X and XII.
[80] *Ibid.*, Part VIII, Chs. XI and XII.

since up till now Levin has felt that, whenever he tried to work for the good of humanity or for the whole village, the activity was unsatisfactory, but that, when he lived more narrowly for himself, he knew his work was necessary. Evidently his conversion will not make him another Koznyshev, whose concern for the general welfare is the result of reasoning,[81] and reasoning which is finally shown to be superficial and false.

Deliberate ambiguity seems to lie in Tolstoy's discussion here of the relation of reason and faith. Besides the assertion that the understanding of goodness is always the same for everyone, Levin uses two unexpected analogies to present to himself the belief he now accepts. He says that, although he *knows* the sky to be limitless space, he is indubitably right when he sees a firm blue vault, and that, although he *knows* that the stars do not move, yet not being able to imagine the rotation of the earth, he is right in saying that they do.[82] To complete the analogy one would say that we are right to acknowledge that God is manifest in the law of goodness which is revealed to men, in spite of what we know to the contrary. What is meant is that, like Pierre, Levin has thrown away his mental telescope and finds the truth at his feet.

A fault in *Anna Karenina* is that Levin's conversion is not adequately integrated into the body of the novel, but is a kind of epilogue. Apart from the account of his praying at the birth of his child, the Levin sections of Parts VI and VII deal with quite other matters than his religious searchings. Levin is perplexed and, before his marriage, depressed; but there is not enough of "the Arzamas misery" in him for it to be intelligible why he should be drawn towards suicide. That he is in danger of killing himself is something we are told but it is not vividly realised; more emphasis is placed on his cutting a definite path for himself through life without knowing why he is doing so. The ultimate impression produced by the novel is the contrast between the wretchedness of Anna's death and the joy of Levin's discovery, though these two things are a long way apart.

[81] *Anna Karenina*, Part III, Ch. I.
[82] *Ibid.*, Part VIII, Chs. XIII and XIX.

6 *Tolstoy's Conversion*

The feeling that the lives led most of the time by people such as Karenin are not "real life" and that, like Levin, one must share the labour of the peasants to live, becomes an explicit thesis in the *Confession*. But one quality Levin does not have in common with Tolstoy is the latter's consuming sense of guilt, which was essential to his conversion, since it told him that there could be no truth in the life of a social parasite.

Tolstoy's sense of guilt had both personal and social aspects, and both are stressed in *The Memoirs of a Madman*. The "madman" condemns his vicious, idle and self-indulgent past. He points out that, when he was passing through Arzamas, he was on his way to buy an estate cheaply from a fool who did not understand business. When he suffered the agony in Moscow, he prayed as if balancing accounts with God and blaming Him, and it was useless. It is only the last time he experiences the misery that he finds it is impossible to present one's account to God, implores forgiveness and remembers his sins. This is the beginning of the "madman's" conversion— which is almost completed on an occasion when he finds that he does not want to buy an estate because the advantages he would get would be based on the peasants' destitution; then he realises that the peasants are his brothers and is glad.

Tolstoy's self-contempt is probably connected with the suicidal urge that appeared in him in the 1870's. The "madman" said, "It is myself I am weary of and find intolerable and a torment." Tolstoy was always prone to self-condemnation, and in the *Confession* this tendency is conspicuous: "Lying, robbery, adultery of all kinds, drunkenness, violence, murder— there was no crime I did not commit."[83] But the point is that, when he did these things, he was following the standards of the aristocratic society in which he had been brought up, and it therefore became necessary for him to free himself from that society. At any rate, his proposition is defensible that one cannot expect to understand the truth about life unless one works and recognises that men cannot live if they do not

[83] *Confession*, II.

co-operate.[84] But at the same time he considered it necessary to share the faith of the peasants, seeing that it made it possible for them to be content with a life of heavy labour and to accept illness, sorrow, and death without opposition—in which respect they were unlike the intellectual who found life meaningless.[85] Accordingly in the *Confession* the contrast is developed between Tolstoy himself, as a representative of a corrupt class, and the Russian peasants, who resemble the mass of mankind, and the point is made that it is only the life of the rich and leisured that is evil; and all his despair is accounted for as being due to sin.

Such a contrast, as Sir Isaiah Berlin has pointed out,[86] occurs repeatedly in the novels and stories. Uncle Eroshka is a more harmonious being than Olenin; Pierre Bezukhov wants to become like the simple soldiers and learn from them, as Levin learns from the peasants; and Gerasim and Nikita, contented and humble people, offset the selfishness of their masters, Ivan Ilych and Vasili Andreevich. Believing, then, that there is another kind of life, which is in harmony with nature, accords with eternal values and with the will of God and makes possible independence and moral freedom, Tolstoy strove to exchange his condition for it. Condemning his mental pride, he accepted the ideas of God, of the divinity of the soul, and of moral goodness and evil, although he said they failed to stand reason's criticism. He simply had no right to deny them and could not live without them.[87] Not only were they the essence of the peasants' wisdom, but they were the beliefs of his own childhood—an innocent and joyful period when he learnt "the spiritual delight of love".[88]

The most emotional and inward aspect of Tolstoy's search for God is presented in *Confession*, XII. Wanting to acknowledge that there is a force in whose power he was, he accepted the argument for the First Cause, but could not conceive his relation with the God he imagined—Creator in Three Persons—de-

---

[84] *Confession*, XI.
[85] *Ibid.*, X.
[86] "Tolstoy and Enlightenment", *Encounter*, Vol. XVI (Feb. 1961.)
[87] *Confession*, IX.
[88] Chiefly from his aunt, Tatiana Alexandrovna; see *Recollections*, written in 1902 and 1908.

tached from the world and himself. Describing his feeling of fear and isolation, he compared himself to a fledgling fallen from its nest, crying for the mother that hatched and reared it. He found then that he was continually alternating between despair and animation, the former condition accompanying his periods of disbelief in God, and the latter his periods of belief. This seemed decisive: to despair was to die; without God he could not live. "To know God and to live is one and the same thing."[89] Therefore he returned to the belief that the aim of life is to live in accord with the Will that produced him and demanded something of him.

In spite of a temporary abasement of reason, he could not accept a faith by which, in order to understand the meaning of life, he must renounce his reason, since reason is the very thing for which alone a meaning is required.[90] But to ask what the meaning of life is, is to ask a question reason cannot answer: it is in itself to attempt to relate the finite to the infinite, and, therefore, to appeal to faith. Tolstoy was asking what meaning his life, as an entity in time and space, had in relation to that which is beyond time and space—the infinite. But the whole concept of the meaning of life (*"smysl zhizni"*) is uncertain. As God, if He exists, is incomprehensible, we cannot expect to know what our lives *mean* to Him, except by revelation. In Tolstoy the search for meaning is, rather, the expression of the desire to relate his life to eternity and to ascribe to it such an aim, resulting from that relation, as will take away the fear of death. Indeed, the search is followed by the joyful assertion that the infinite is in us, and that we have a relationship with God, not as mere creatures required to obey Him, but as a part of Him, able to transcend space and time and live in Him—an assertion which, with the deductions that follow from it, and together with the belief that the desire

[89] This part of the *Confession* is laboriously attacked by Plekhanov, who points out that the argument assumes as proved the very thing that it is required to prove: the existence of God; for from the statement that I live only when I believe in God's existence, the only thing that follows is that I myself cannot live without belief in God. Plekhanov emphasises the influence on Tolstoy, at the time of his conversion, of the beliefs of his childhood.—"From Here to Here" (*"Otsyuda i dosyuda"*), 1910, I, reprinted in *L. N. Tolstoy v russkoy kritike, Sbornik statey*, ed. S. P. Bychkov.

[90] *Confession*, VIII.

for personal well-being has to be renounced, is held to be a
sufficient statement of the meaning of life. Tolstoy writes:

> The simplest labouring people around me were the Russian
> people, and I turned to them and to the meaning of life which
> they give. That meaning, if one can put it into words, was as
> follows: Every man has come into this world by the will of God.
> And God has so made man that every man can destroy his soul
> or save it. The aim of man in life is to save his soul, and to save
> his soul he must live 'godly' and to live 'godly' he must re-
> nounce all the pleasures of life, must labour, humble himself,
> suffer, and be merciful.[91]

Such a meaning is what Tolstoy needed, for it includes the
necessary aim (*"zadacha"*)—that of saving one's soul and seeking God, living in accord with His will, and renouncing the
vain pleasures of the realm that death rules. When Pierre
Bezukhov is converted, he is no longer concerned about the
aim (*"tsel'* ") of life, having found God; but Tolstoy, after his
conversion, was continually trying to clarify that aim. This
was not only to provide a rational support for his characteristic
tendency to strive for moral perfection, but also to emancipate
himself, bit by bit, from everything death could destroy. Like
Prince Andrew, by approaching the divine he would overcome
the fear of death.

In Chapter v of the *Confession*, where Tolstoy describes his
despair and his search for the meaning of life, he considers the
conclusions of metaphysics, which are in contrast with the distressing materialism of his day; and he writes:

> Whether the philosopher calls the essence of life existing within
> me, and in all that exists, by the name of 'idea', or 'substance',
> or 'spirit', or 'will', he says one and the same thing: that this
> essence exists and that I am of that same essence; but why it is
> he does not know, and does not say, if he is an exact thinker. I
> ask: 'Why should this essence exist? What results from the
> fact that it is and will be?' ... And philosophy not merely does
> not reply, but is itself only asking that question.

"The essence of life" (*"sushchnost' zhizni"*) is the very phrase
that was used at the end of *War and Peace*, when a metaphysical

---

[91] *Confession*, XIII.

theory was devised as a means of withdrawal from the intolerable position that determinism had landed us in. Now, however, the theory that the essence of life is free is not enough; Tolstoy must go on to find belief in the soul's salvation. Why is this?

Lyubov Axelrod has said[92] that, if one asks why the essence of life exists, one may as well ask:

> Why does God exist? What results from the fact that He is and will be? . . . Why did He send us into the world? Why are we obliged to fulfil His will, which demands from us humility, patience, absolute submission, and rejection of "all the pleasures of life"? And if the pleasures of life are evil, sin and a fall, then why did He create this temptation? . . .

And she comments:

> We see that Tolstoy, who was proud, fundamentally not in the least inclined to humility, and a sceptic to the marrow of his bones, finds complete tranquillity in the worst and most offensive of all dogmas.

The explanation she gives of this is that he was still bound by the religion taught him in childhood, which was the religion of the aristocracy, and that, in spite of his laborious pursuit of perfection, he could never rid himself of the attitudes acquired in childhood, which, as the recollections he wrote at the end of his life show, was a period he always looked back on with pleasure. She says further that he was always suspicious of new ideas, approaching them as an antagonist rather than a seeker, with the result that his destructive criticism turned him back to the world-view of his childhood. Aware of the true nature of social privilege, and convinced that contemporary culture was leading to moral ruin, he saw that the labouring people, who suffered endless deprivation and were not spoilt by contemporary urban culture, fulfilled the precepts of the Gospels and, through their belief in a divine purpose, attained tranquillity.

[92] "Tolstoy's Inner Tragedy as the Basis of his Doctrine" ("*Dushevnaya tragediya Tolstogo, kak osnova ego veroucheniya*"), 1912, VIII, reprinted in *O Tolstom: Literaturno-kriticIhesky sbornik*, ed. V. M. Friche. Cf. Antony Flew, "Tolstoi and the Meaning of Life", *Ethics*, Vol. LXXIII (Jan. 1963).

This is not a complete answer, but later Axelrod says what is necessary and most relevant to the present essay, when she describes Tolstoy's teaching as one "which sees the highest happiness and the summit of moral perfection in destruction of the will to live and slow suicide".[93] The chief horror to Tolstoy was not so much death, as living when death was to follow. Therefore he had a choice between suicide, and convincing himself that he had another, "true" life beyond time and space which death could not touch, and that it was possible to begin now the process that death would eventually complete, of emancipating himself from that "false" life which death would destroy. To make continual effort towards self-renunciation is to progress along the infinite road to perfection, and that is to free oneself from "false" life. "To live rationally one must live so that death cannot destroy life."[94]

To ask the meaning of life is to look for something other than a predetermined process of causally connected events. Reason, in contemplating such a process, had produced for Levin the theory of the struggle for existence, so that a morality based on something beyond that process appeared irrational. But once Tolstoy recognised his belief, which was implicit in his question as to the meaning of life, that there is an infinite Being outside time and space and independent of cause, Christian morality no longer appeared irrational. In this he was helped by Pascal:

> The heart has its reasons of which the reason knows nothing, as we see on a thousand occasions. I say that the heart has a natural love for the Universal Being or for itself, according as it surrenders to the one or the other; and it hardens against either at its own will. You have rejected one and kept the other. Is it reason that makes you love yourself?

This idea forms the basis of Tolstoy's definition of religion.[95]

In the essay *On Life* he tries, as we have seen, to settle the problem that troubled Levin as to the relation between an ethic of love and the law of the struggle for existence. Reason

---

[93] "Tolstoy's Inner Tragedy", XIV. [94] *What I Believe*, VIII.
[95] *Religion and Morality*. Pascal's *Pensées* are translated by J. M. Cohen. Harmondsworth (Penguin), 1961.

discovers such a law when, directed outwards, it studies the animal world, but the law is not applicable to man, who, besides his animal personality, has reason, or reasonable consciousness, a self-sufficient and indefinable entity. The ethics of love and self-sacrifice are proclaimed because all others are allegedly vain, being inconsistent with the dualistic view of human nature. The argument thus depends on the distinction between what is in time and space and what is beyond them.

7 *"The Death of Ivan Ilych"*

The Death of Ivan Ilych was published in 1886. By describing the course of a physical disease and the thoughts of a dying man, Tolstoy was able to transmute into a clear and immediately appreciable artistic form those feelings that he had experienced at Arzamas and in the 1870's, when he seemed to be brought face to face with death. At the same time he is detached from his subject, and makes Ivan Ilych a man unlike himself.

Ivan Ilych is a judge. Like Karenin, he is limited and selfish, leading an artificial life without warmth, and excessively concerned about appearances and propriety. Thanks to his quarrels with his wife, he is reduced to requiring only four things of his marriage: dinner, a housewife, bed, and propriety. In his job he delights in the exercise of power and achieves success, but his aim is always so to maintain official relations with the people he deals with as to exclude everything fresh and vital. He enjoys the pleasures of ambition and of vanity, but, above all, of bridge. In this last respect he resembles Peter Ivanovich and Schwartz, who appear at his house before his funeral; for them bridge is an amusement they can resort to after an unpleasant scene, but for the reader it is a symbol of the frivolity that conceals from them the realities of life and death.

What appears at first to Ivan Ilych as a trivial injury in his side turns out to be the origin of a fatal disease. When he first sees a doctor, the scene is like those in the law courts with which he is familiar; only now it is the doctor who is the judge. The doctor will not enter into human relations with his patient, but is only concerned with diagnosis and treatment. "It was not a question of Ivan Ilych's life or death, but one between a

floating kidney and appendicitis." Ivan Ilych is roused to
fury by every mischance that destroys his peace of mind; and
this fury, and the awareness that his life is poisoned and is
poisoning the lives of others, are the equivalents of the nausea
and spitefulness of Tolstoy's "madman". When he over-
trumps his partner at bridge he finds he does not care, for he
is now alone on the brink of an abyss, where death is being
revealed to him, as real life was revealed to Karenin.

Remorselessly he is brought face to face with "*It*". When,
in the law court, he feels the pain in his side, "*It*" stands before
him; and no consolations—no screens—can conceal "*It*" for
long. "*It*" looks at him from behind the flowers in the drawing-
room, where he received his injury; and he is alone with "*It*"
in his study. "And nothing could be done with *It* except to
look at it and shudder."

He comes to hate his wife on account of her reproaches and
her insincerity. He longs for pity, which only Gerasim, the
butler's assistant, and Vasya, Ivan Ilych's son, have for him.
None of the others will admit that Ivan Ilych is dying, and
he is tormented by the falsity that surrounds him. He likes
Gerasim for his strength and vitality, as well as for his truthfulness. Gerasim is not unduly troubled by the uncleanliness that
offends Ivan Ilych, and nurses his master deftly.

Ivan Ilych weeps like a child. Helpless and lonely, he asks
God why he is suffering, not expecting an answer. He asks
himself what he wants, and replies, "To live as I used to—well
and pleasantly." But, on consideration, he finds that his only
genuinely pleasant memories are those of childhood, and that,
as he grew up, his joys became more and more dubious:

> It is as if I had been going downhill while I imagined I was
> going up. And that is really what it was. I was going up in
> public opinion, but to the same extent life was ebbing away
> from me.

This is a familiar theme in Tolstoy, but here the didacticism
obtrudes: Ivan Ilych's thought that perhaps he did not live
as he ought to have done is declared to be "the sole solution of
all the riddles of life and death". Ivan Ilych, however, rejects
it, pleading "Not guilty".

But the thought recurs to him: his life grew worse and worse, like his illness. "There is one bright spot there at the back, at the beginning of life, and afterwards all becomes blacker and blacker . . ." Life is a series of increasing sufferings that culminates in death. Later he suddenly wonders, "What if my whole life has really been wrong?" and finds it so wrong that there is nothing to defend. What might have been right— "the real thing"—was only his scarcely perceptible attempt to oppose the moral standards of people of his class; his professional duties, his family life, and his social and official interests he sees were not real at all, "but a terrible and huge deception which had hidden both life and death."

He begins to scream and screams for three days, returning to a dream he had before. He imagines he is being thrust into a black sack, struggling helplessly. This is painful, but even more so is his not being able to get right into it, which is due to his conviction that his life was a good one. His justification of his life is holding him back and tormenting him. But suddenly he falls through the hole, and there at the bottom is light. The moment he sees the light is the moment his schoolboy son kisses his hand and begins to cry. Ivan Ilych recognises finally that his life was "not the right thing"; for, as with the "madman", no release from torment is possible until he acknowledges his sins. Immediately he feels sorry for his son and even for his wife, wanting, for the first time, to release them from suffering; and he acknowledges God, "knowing that He whose understanding mattered would understand" what he is trying to say to his wife when asking forgiveness. The physical pain continues, but there is no more fear of death, for "in place of death there was light. 'So that's what it is!' he suddenly exclaimed aloud. 'What joy!' " And he dies.

His being thrust into that sack is similar to death pushing the door open in Prince Andrew's dream. Both Andrew and Ivan Ilych resist, but when they are overcome they feel an inner liberation. Ivan Ilych's conviction that his life had been a good one bound him to life, as Andrew was bound by his love for Natasha. The light at the bottom of the hole is the bright spot at the beginning of Ivan Ilych's life; it is the pure joy experienced in early childhood and accessible again when everything else is renounced. His life has been so selfish that to admit that it was wrong is to repudiate everything except that bright spot. But, whereas with Andrew the divine love which is discovered belongs to another realm and has no object, Ivan Ilych, when he sees the light, feels sorry for his son and his wife. Yet this pity is not a feeling that makes him want to live, as Andrew wanted to live when he loved Natasha, but it makes him desire death, in order to release his son and his wife from the suffering he is causing them.

The inner resemblance between *The Death of Ivan Ilych* and the *Confession* consists not only in the similarity of the awareness of the approach of death and the concomitant bitterness and despair, and not only in the fact that Gerasim, as a representative of the peasants, is a sane and vital man, not daunted by the thought of death, but also in the importance in both works of the recognition of guilt and of the consequent asceticism. Philip Rahv says:

> The disease which ravages Ilyich evidently represents Tolstoy's reaction against the natural world with which he formerly identified himself and his advance toward a rational religiosity and an ethical conception of social existence.[96]

There is a scene in which Ivan Ilych is indignant at the sight of his daughter in evening dress ("making a show of that very flesh which in his own case caused so much suffering"), and simultaneously enraged by his family's inane conversation about Sarah Bernhardt; that display of flesh is associated with the false values and frivolity of the class to which Ivan Ilych belongs. Ivan Ilych has scarcely known what life is; the kind of sensuality that is repudiated here is far from the primitive and vital sensuality of *The Cossacks*. His death is the tormenting end of a narrow and sterile existence; yet this harrowing destruction of a man's body leads inevitably to the same conclusion that Tolstoy, the great artist of nature, reached in the contemplation of death. This conclusion, the discovery of an inner light and a sense of liberation from the body, had been

---

[96] "The Death of Ivan Ilyich and Joseph K.", 2, *Image and Idea*, pp. 132-3. Norfolk, Conn. (New Directions) 1957.

prefigured in the death of Prince Andrew; it is the essence of Tolstoy's dualism; and is now expressed in the most disciplined and concentrated prose, with an intensity derived from that fierce sense of guilt which made Tolstoy renounce his former existence.

Professor Rahv emphasises the question of social status in Tolstoy, saying that his conversion was prompted by the breakdown of the ancient patriarchal relations, and the protest of the bewildered peasantry and nobility against the transformation of Russia into a capitalist country. Ivan Ilych is the average man of the city.

> And as to the mysterious catastrophe which destroys Ilyich, what is it in historical reality if not the ghost of the old idealism of status returning to avenge itself on its murderer?

Whatever may be meant by the phrase "historical reality", this is the sort of interpretation that obscures as much as it reveals, by reducing a thing to the level of one of its conditions. But it is necessary to point out the difference in social standing between Ivan Ilych, on the one hand, and Pierre, Andrew, Levin, and Tolstoy himself on the other. Professor Rahv speaks of the "characterlessness" of Ivan Ilych; he is unheroic, exemplifying the "historic depletion of man" that is connected with nineteenth-century capitalism,[97] whereas Andrew and Levin are proud and independent, Levin shares some of his creator's vigour, and Pierre, too, has individuality—all qualities due, to some extent at least, to their aristocratic status.

Clearly Tolstoy was bewildered by the new forces in Russian society, and in his last, religious period he created no characters, except for Hadji Murad, with that fulness of being of the Rostovs or Anna Karenina. The mordant scorn that runs through *Resurrection* is poles apart from the genial warmth of parts of *War and Peace*. And when Tolstoy expresses his religious consciousness in the artistic works of his last period, he does so through the characterless Ivan Ilych, the equally anonymous Vasili Andreevich, a merchant, the degraded Nikita of *The Power of Darkness*, and the depraved Nekhlyudov of *Resurrection*, a representative of a very decadent aristocracy. It is as though,

[97] *Ibid.*, 2, pp. 135 and 138.

F

in the struggle of the spirit against nature, Tolstoy, in choosing these personages, refuses to give nature a chance; his own animal strength is saved for Hadji Murad. In the works to be examined next, *The Power of Darkness* and *Master and Man*, there is the austerity and the preoccupation with guilt that characterise the *Confession* and *The Death of Ivan Ilych*, and the irruption of a spiritual force demanding self-sacrifice, which has here as its antagonists, not the old bear-like Tolstoyan strength and natural fecundity, but, in Vasili Andreevich as in Ivan Ilych, ordinary selfishness, and, in Nikita, the fear and despair of a murderer.

8 "The Power of Darkness"

In the same year as *The Death of Ivan Ilych*, *The Power of Darkness* was written. It is a realistic play; and, although Tolstoy risks a few monologues, on the whole he has to rely on dialogue and action to convey the feelings and insights, which in his novels could be communicated by tracing the inmost thoughts of his protagonists.

The play has the moral, "If a claw is caught the bird is lost." Nikita, a labourer, is ruined by his lasciviousness, not realising the net of evil into which it is leading him, and by his weakness in submitting to the two terrible women, Matrëna, his mother, and Anisya, who drive him to murder. The whole of Act I demonstrates that, if only he would obey his father, Akim, and leave Anisya so as to marry Marina, whom he has seduced, he would be saved. Crossing himself before the icon, he swears that there has been nothing between him and Marina. From that moment he is lost. The pious old cesspool-cleaner has said that you can hide the truth from men but not from God.

Akim, hardly articulate but impressively humble, represents the traditional wisdom of the Russian peasant. Matrëna, on the other hand, seems to be completely evil. In Act II she induces Anisya to poison her husband, Peter, Nikita's employer, and to steal his money, so that Nikita and Anisya together may possess the homestead. Nikita, "so tender-hearted . . . he usen't to be able to kill a chicken", is not told about the powders, and he weeps when Peter Ignatich, as is customary before dying, asks for forgiveness. But he is made an accomplice by being given the money to hide.

Act III shows Nikita, apparently tired of Anisya, turning to Akulina, his wife's stupid step-daughter, and the two women are bitterly jealous. Akim walks out, refusing his son's hospitality, disgusted with Nikita's drunkenness and the women's quarrel. As Shaw said in a letter to Tolstoy:

> The preaching of the old man, right as he was, could never be of any use—it could only anger his son and rub the last grains of self-respect out of him.[98]

In Act IV Nikita, degraded further, is urged by Anisya and Matrëna to murder the child he has had by Akulina so that Akulina may marry and they be rid of her. It appears that Nikita now knows of the murder of Peter Ignatich and hates Anisya for it:

> She's made me her partner in these horrors—that jade! . . . She became loathsome, loathsome to me as soon as mother told me about it.

Remorselessly the women compel him to murder the infant; and he is horrified:

> How it began to whimper, and how the little bones crunched . . . krr . . . I'm not a man now!

Act V, Scene I, is the scene that Shaw especially admired, in which a drunken soldier, Mitrich, having interfered with Nikita's attempt at hanging himself, wallows with him in the straw, and, by telling Nikita not to fear men, "as if he was the voice of God" does what the pious Akim could not do. Nikita goes directly to the hut where everyone is assembled waiting for him to give his blessing to Akulina's wedding. He enters with his father, falls on his knees and confesses. He even confesses to a crime he has not committed—the murder of Peter Ignatich. Everyone is astonished; Matrëna and Anisya try to make him get up, saying he is mad or bewitched, and a police officer attempts to make an arrest. In the midst, Akim is exultant:

> God will forgive you, my own son! You have had no mercy on yourself, He will show mercy on you! God—God! It is He!

[98] Quoted by Aylmer Maude in *The Life of Tolstoy*, Vol. II, Ch. XVII, p. 462.

The impressive title of the play suggests that the evil in question is not just Nikita's or Anisya's or Matrëna's, but is, as Dr Steiner remarks,[99] a general bestiality growing out of the ignorance of the Russian peasants. Old Akim complained that God had been forgotten. Nikita gave himself easily to the power of darkness that surrounds him, but, unlike Matrëna and Anisya, felt miserable and degraded on account of his tender-heartedness and the shreds of conscience that remained to him. His sense of guilt drove him to suicide, so that, when Mitrich saves him, he has nothing more to lose. But it is better to "spit in the devil's beard" then to die in shame. The desperate nature of his confession is shown by his claiming to have poisoned Peter Ignatich. In one sense, by his confession he is still trying to do himself in, having failed with a rope; in another, by overcoming his fear and begging forgiveness, he is restoring himself before his conscience and in the eyes of his father. As with Ivan Ilych, everything must be renounced so that the light may shine.

George Steiner makes the acute remark that "the climax moves beyond realism into a mood of tragic ritual", but he does not develop the point. In *The Idea of a Theater* [100] Francis Fergusson demonstrates that in *Hamlet*, besides Ophelia's funeral, there are scenes of royal pageantry which have ritual significance in that they invoke a divinely established social order with the king as the head, but which turn out to be tragic failures because of the presence of the evil that they cannot conceal. Similarly Akulina's wedding is a tragic failure. Traditional religion is invoked throughout the play, not only in the words of Akim, but also in Peter Ignatich's request for forgiveness, and in the presence of icons and the sign of the cross. But Nikita forswears himself; Peter Ignatich's request comes when he is being murdered; and a girl remarks that Akulina, who is marrying only because Nikita told her to, omitted the customary lamentation over the approaching loss of her maidenhood. The supreme irony comes when Nikita is required to give the blessing: on his knees before them, he disrupts the wedding by revealing the evil that till then has been hidden,

[99] *Tolstoy or Dostoevsky*, Ch. 2, vii, p. 128.
[100] Princeton, N.J. (Princeton University Press), 1949, Ch. 4.

but at the same time asserts those religious values that are being betrayed before him. The external religious elements in the play become a travesty of religious belief, but co-existent with them is an inner movement of sin and expiation, by which such belief is ultimately vindicated.

9 "*Master and Man*"

Master and Man (written in 1895) is as detailed a study of peasant life as Tolstoy's early story *Polikushka*; and the sensations of travelling in a blinding snowstorm are as distinctly and minutely realised in it as they are in the early semi-autobiographical story *The Snow Storm*.

Vasili Andreevich, a merchant, set out with a peasant, Nikita, to buy a grove. Like Tolstoy passing through Arzamas, he is on his way to do a profitable piece of business when he encounters death. As Ivan Ilych was forestalled by a fatal illness just when he seemed to be embarking on a new period of success, so Vasili Andreevich, of whose life money-making constituted "the sole aim, meaning, pleasure and pride", lies awake in his sledge reckoning the profit he will make on the grove, congratulating himself on the wealth he has already amassed, and envying the millionaire, Mironov, while all around him, in the "fluctuating whity darkness", the wind is blowing and piling the snow up round the sledge, the horse, and Nikita. The bleakness of the night in the open is intensified by comparison with the warmth and hospitality of the house at Grishkino, where they were invited to stay the night. Vasili Andreevich refused the invitation because of his anxiety to buy the grove before anyone else could. When they got lost after leaving Grishkino, it was Nikita who recognised that they would have to spend the night in the open. Vasili Andreevich now blames himself for listening to Nikita, and grows more and more afraid. Shivering, he climbs out of the sledge and clambers on to the horse, to ride away leaving Nikita alone, thinking:

> It's all the same to him whether he lives or dies. What is his life worth? . . .

Nikita, a habitual drunkard whom Vasili Andreevich employs cheaply and tries to cheat, but a kindly man, is not particularly frightened by death, because his life has been one of ceaseless toil of which he is weary, and because he believes that after death he will still be dependent on his other Master, God, Who will not ill-use him.

When Vasili Andreevich is alone on the horse, his terror increases, and it is at its greatest when the horse sinks into a snowdrift and he is left alone in the snow. He prays, being a church-warden, but only realises the irrelevance of his formal religion. Running forward, he suddenly sees the horse standing beside the sledge, and it turns out that, in spite of his attempts to reach the grove, the horse was merely bringing him back to the sledge.

By the time Vasili Andreevich sees Nikita lying in the sledge, his terror has left him; but Nikita is dying. Vasili Andreevich, "with the same resolution with which he used to strike hands when making a good purchase", rakes the snow off Nikita and lies face down on top of his servant, covering him with his coat and the whole of his body. He grows tearful, experiencing "a peculiar joy such as he had never felt before". His hands and legs begin to freeze, but he thinks only of how to keep Nikita warm. Various impressions and recollections fill his mind, and he falls asleep. He dreams he is lying in bed and must get up, because the police officer is soon going to call on him.

> Then suddenly his joy was completed. He whom he was expecting came; not Ivan Matveich the police officer, but some-one else—yet it was he whom he had been waiting for. He came and called him; and it was he who had called him and told him to lie down on Nikita.

Vasili Andreevich wakes up, but is unable to move; "and it seemed to him that he was Nikita and Nikita was he, and that his life was not in himself but in Nikita". His financial undertakings seem now to have belonged to someone else—Vasili—who " 'did not know what the real thing was . . . but now I know and know for sure . . .' And again he heard the voice of the one who had called him before." He answers gladly, "I'm coming!" and, feeling free, he dies.

Vasili Andreevich's decision to save Nikita is unexpected,

as is his joy. His life had the same narrowness and selfishness as Ivan Ilych's, and, when the horse leads him back to Nikita, he is virtually defeated; but, whereas Ivan Ilych had to choose between justification of himself and acknowledgment of sin, between protesting against death and consenting to the inevitable. Vasili Andreevich suddenly chooses to save another regardless of his own life. Just as pity and the light of innocence revealed to Ivan Ilych that his life was not the right thing, so Vasili Andreevich learns that his life was not the real thing, in his almost physical blending with Nikita.

The mystery why Vasili Andreevich sacrifices himself for Nikita, Tolstoy develops in the account of the dream, with the mysterious "someone else" who told Vasili Andreevich to lie on Nikita, and whom he continues to acknowledge after waking up. The explicit reference to God in *The Death of Ivan Ilych* appears incidentally; here a new realm is revealed to Vasili as to Prince Andrew; only instead of the abstract phrasing of Andrew's last meditations, there is here a personal image. "He" bade Vasili Andreevich preserve Nikita and summons him from this life. The irony is that the pious Nikita, on being found the next morning, is sorry still to be alive, and, when he dies twenty years later, he is glad to do so.

The discoveries that are made by Ivan Ilych and Vasili Andreevich are not mere formulae presented as interior monologue, though such monologue is essential to the author's purpose. Rather, the "light" and the mysterious "someone" are images that serve as focal points of the complete stories, of which Tolstoy needs the whole to express his awareness of revelation, just as the meaning of *The Power of Darkness* does not lie merely in Mitrich's words to Nikita or in Akim's understanding of Nikita's confession, but in what the drama is, its whole movement. These images symbolise an internal realm not subject to observation, but are meaningless without the stories in which they occur and which describe the defeat of the pursuit of personal well-being. The solution, self-sacrifice and the life of the spirit, is given to those who, like Tolstoy at Arzamas, have experienced that defeat or, like Nikita in *The Power of Darkness*, are ruined by guilt. For Prince Andrew life and happiness were compatible only in rare moments. Levin, a good-natured man, suffered despair when already close to the peasants, though he was not close to them in his thinking till after his conversion. The God Who is now revealed, unlike the immanent Deity discovered by Pierre Bezukhov, is manifest only in such love as Vasili Andreevich showed the dying Nikita. But the characters that have the (artistically) best achieved wholeness and oneness with life, Hadji Murad and Uncle Eroshka, do not know such love.

10 The Death of Hadji Murad

Hadji Murad was written at intervals between 1896 and 1904, and published posthumously. It is another tale of the war in the Caucasus, like those Tolstoy wrote in the 1850's, but differs from them in that it has no central character who resembles Tolstoy and who judges events. As in *The Cossacks*, however, a comparison emerges between civilisation and nature. The Russians are represented as coarse, self-indulgent, and senselessly cruel; the Tartars are energetic, fierce, poetic, and austere; nevertheless there is a sympathetic portrayal of Marya Dmitrievna, an officer's mistress, and Hadji Murad's enemy, Shamil, appears in a bad light. Some scenes are well done, but there is a thinness about others, showing that they required to be rewritten. Chapters xxiii and xxv, however, which are the most relevant to this study, are among the most vivid pieces of writing in Tolstoy.

The theme is stated at the beginning in the comparison of Hadji Murad to a thistle; determined and, in spite of his coming over to the Russians, morally independent, he defends himself to the end, having his own inalienable right to life, his own beauty and his own vitality. He is brave and gentle. The "terrible mountain chief" surprises and delights both Poltoratsky and Marya Vasilevna with the childlike kindliness of his smile; but a different image of him is given when he appears at Tiflis, limping briskly into the general's waiting-room, and standing with his hand on his dagger, looking round contemptuously at all those present. The autobiography he gives the aide-de-camp contains feats of great daring, but also

tender recollections of his mother.[101] His dexterity in dealing
with the surprise attack by Arslan Khan bears out the impression of his heroism; and in Chapter xxiii, when his murids
are preparing the weapons for escape, Khanefi is singing, and
Hadji Murad is meditating, listening to Khanefi and to the
ecstatic songs of the nightingales, and recalling his last conversation with his son, the handsome, tall Yusuf, the association
of beauty and courage is complete.
The nightingales sing again in the last scene, though their
songs are hushed while the firing lasts. After attempting to
escape from the Russians, Hadji Murad has to entrench himself
with his few followers among some shrubs, where he is surrounded by his foes. After shooting unerringly, he is eventually
wounded. Lying in the ditch, he knows that he is dying, and
memories and pictures flash through his mind.

> All these images passed through his mind without evoking any
> feeling within him—neither pity nor anger nor any kind of
> desire: everything seemed so insignificant in comparison with
> what was beginning, or had already begun, within him.

But he rises from the ditch, shoots another attacker, and limping
heavily goes dagger in hand at the foe. Again he is shot down,
and with triumphant shrieks his enemies rush towards him.
But he suddenly moves, clinging to the trunk of a tree.

> He seemed so terrible, that those who were running towards
> him stopped short. But suddenly a shudder passed through
> him, he staggered away from the tree and fell on his face,
> stretched out at full length like a thistle that had been mown
> down, and he moved no more.
> He did not move, but still he felt.
> When Hadji Aga, who was the first to reach him, struck
> him on the head with a large dagger, it seemed to Hadji Murad
> that someone was striking him with a hammer and he could
> not understand who was doing it or why. That was his last
> consciousness of any connexion with his body. He felt nothing

---

[101] Maude puts these recollections in Chapter xi. It is more usual to find them
in Chapter xxiii.

more and his enemies kicked and hacked at what had no longer anything in common with him.

Two things are done here. The terrible beauty that Hadji Murad has had in his life is there still in his death, in his dying body, as it is in the severed head that is displayed in the forts and villages—"Notwithstanding the many wounds on the head, the blue lips still bore a kindly childlike expression"—and at the same time the Tolstoyan spirituality is hinted at, but only negatively: the seeming insignificance of everything that concerned Hadji Murad in his lifetime is an echo of the thoughts of the dying Vasili Andreevich, and the last two sentences in the quotation above are a reference to the theory of immortality propounded in the essay *On Life*. But whereas Vasili Andreevich, like Ivan Ilych, was attached to life by narrow, selfish aims, Hadji Murad has always rejoiced in a freshness and full-bloodedness; and whereas Vasili repudiated his money-making in his last moments, and Ivan Ilych a career of petty ambition, the pictures that present themselves to Hadji Murad, as he is dying, are not only of his adventures but of his wife and son—of Yusuf, whose face and figure "breathed of daring, youth and the joy of life". What Hadji Murad is deprived of in death *is* "the real thing", as far as the story goes —and that qualification is necessary, as his Mohammedanism is looked at only from the outside, and the consolation it might provide him with is not realised. Instead, Tolstoy hints at his own doctrine, but affirms nothing except the independence of the conscious self from the body.

> What man fears is not death, which he does not know, but life, which his animal and rational existence alone know. The feeling which is expressed in men by the fear of death is nothing but the consciousness of an intrinsic contradiction of life. . .
>
> The best proof that the fear of death is not in reality a fear of death but of false life, is that people often kill themselves from that very fear. Men are horrified at the thought of death not because they fear that their life may end with it, but because physical death clearly shows them the necessity of the true life which they do not possess.[102]

[102] *On Life*, xxvii.

This, a rationalisation of Tolstoy's own experience, could be applied, too, to the cases of Ivan Ilych and Vasili Andreevich, who experienced the contradiction of life in the denial of their personal pleasure and the defeat of their aims, and who, in their last moments, discovered that "true life", which, consisting in self-sacrifice and an immortal consciousness, overcomes death but ascribes no value to physical existence. Hadji Murad, however, like Uncle Eroshka, is aware of no such contradiction. He admits having been afraid of death, but, being ashamed of that fear, which is, anyway, different from the obsessive dread of Ivan Ilych or "the Arzamas misery", he makes it an element in his courage. He dies bravely a death that is the result of his own miscalculations and of the tragic complexity of events.[103] And in the account of his dying the protest is implicit which is made explicit at the beginning of the story, when, contemplating the thistle, Tolstoy laments man's destructiveness.

11 Conclusion

In conclusion it may be said that there is a specific theme in Tolstoy that appears in Olenin's desire to live for others as he wants nothing for himself, and that reaches its fullest expression in the death of Vasili Andreevich. In opposition to this is a powerful awareness of natural beauty and vigour, and a desire for fulness of being—a desire that finds expression in the portrayal of strong, primitive characters like Eroshka and Hadji Murad, and that is manifest at other times in a vague craving for mystical unity in life: Olenin's nature-mysticism, Karataev's wholeness and roundedness, and Pierre's tranquillity.

[103] When Tolstoy mentioned in a letter to his brother Sergey, on 23 December 1851, that Hadji Murad had surrendered to the Russians, he described the action as "mean". (Quoted by Aylmer Maude in *The Life of Tolstoy*, Vol. I, Ch. III, p. 69.) Moral condemnation of Hadji Murad is perhaps implied in the story. A weakness is that the cause of his final breach with Shamil is not made clear (XIII); but Chapter XVII, which gives an account of the ruined state of a village the Russians destroyed—that very village where Hadji Murad had stayed before going over to the Russians—contains such an eloquent expression of the loathing felt by the Chechens for the Russians, that it seems nothing could justify Hadji Murad's joining the latter to fight the Mohammedan tribes. Moreover, Hadji Murad's shooting, in his escape from the Russians, of the Cossack Nazarov—"a young, healthy . . . lad, as fresh as a rose"—is more callous than the killing of Hadji Murad himself.

But this craving for unity yields too vague a conclusion to satisfy that insistent seeking for the meaning of life, which, combined with a consuming sense of guilt and corrosive despair, is ultimately the desire to transfer life to a region beyond time and space and overcome death, and which ensures the final triumph in Tolstoy of religious dogma and metaphysical dualism.

III

God

Let us now look at the precise nature of Tolstoy's doctrine concerning God, consciousness, the self, and the personality. The previous chapter has shown that he had to believe in God in order to save himself from despair and the thought of an inevitable death, and indeed after his conversion he acquired new resolution and purposefulness. Moreover, he was able in three marvellous works of art to create personages who, like himself and unlike his brother Nicholas, found something to cling to when in the presence of death. "Behold, I show you a mystery!" say these works of art. But if there is mystery, and not mystification, how can there be a theology? Tolstoy wanted a universal explanatory principle; as at the time of writing *War and Peace* an explanation was needed for the baffling movement of history, so in the 1880's an explanation was needed to account for his own, and Ivan Ilych's, death and resurrection, and to show that this is the general law of life.

When he quarrelled with the Orthodox Church and came to the conclusion that the dogmas of all the churches were harmful nonsense, except in so far as they confirmed his own metaphysic and teaching of love, he had to fix the limits of reason very carefully. Using an illustration taken from Pascal, he wrote early in the 1880's:

> I call revelation that which opens out to us, when reason has reached its utmost limits, the contemplation of what is divine, that is, of truth that is superior to our reason. I call revelation that which gives an answer to the question, insoluble by reason, which brought me to despair and almost to suicide—the question: What meaning has my life? That answer must be intelligible and must not contradict the laws of reason as would, for instance, the assertion that an infinite number is odd or even.

It must not contradict reason, for I shall not believe an answer that does so, and it must be intelligible and not arbitrarily assumed, but inevitable to one's reason as, for instance, a recognition of infinity is to any man who is able to count. The answer must reply to the question: What meaning has my life? A reply that does not answer that question is useless to me. The answer must be such that though its essence may be incomprehensible in itself (as is the essence of God) all the deductions derived from its consequences should correspond to every demand of reason, and the meaning it ascribes to my life should solve all my questions as to how to live. The answer must be not merely reasonable and clear but also true, that is, such as I can believe in with my whole soul inevitably, as I believe in the existence of infinity.[1]

There is truth, then, which is superior to reason—and in this context "reason" should be understood as the power of discursive reasoning, rather than the absolute reasonable consciousness, or intuitive reason, of *On Life*. But the answer given by revelation must not contradict reason; and in Chapter VII of *What is Religion ?*, which was finished in 1902, Tolstoy is still insisting that the assertions of true faith, though they cannot be proved, never contain anything contrary to reason or incompatible with human knowledge. But what presents a problem is that, although the answer given by revelation cannot by definition be discovered by reason, yet it must be inevitable to reason and not arbitrarily assumed. Especially when one is trying to find an answer to a question such as: What meaning has my life? it is easy to make mere assertions about the nature of God, which can be neither proved nor refuted, or which, being arbitrary affirmations, may be arbitrarily denied. To show that Tolstoy adopted certain propositions about the nature of God and of life because he wanted to do so in order to live and not kill himself, is not, of course, to refute those propositions; but it may be possible to indicate that they are not inevitable to one's reason.

2 *The Self and God*

According to Aylmer Maude,

Tolstoy prayed regularly and ardently, but he did not believe

---

[1] *Introduction to an Examination of the Gospels.*

in a personal God—that is to say, he was not prepared to make definite statements on a matter he could not verify. . . .

Owing to the limitations of human thought and language, Tolstoy found that in practice he used a more personal note in his prayers than in a philosophic argument he would have been inclined to defend.[2]

In his diaries there are both the personal note of his prayers and speculation as to the nature of God. Dr Steiner notes:

> Time and again, as in his diary for May 1896, he referred to "this God who is enclosed in man". The very existence of God appears to have been acceptable to him only in terms of human identity.[3]

What Dr Steiner means by human identity is not clear, for he does not raise Tolstoy's distinction between self and personality. However, he continues:

> In the main, Tolstoy was obsessed with reason and a desire for clear understanding. The part of Voltaire in him was too prominent to accept for very long shadowy intimations of the divine presence. If God existed, He was "other" than man. . . .

There are two possibilities. One is that God is other than man. But recognition of such a God would at least not be inevitable to one's reason in the same sense as a recognition of infinity is to any man who can count. Pascal said that, as we are finite and have extension, and God has neither extension nor limits, He bears no relation to us and is incomprehensible, so that we cannot even know whether He exists. Tolstoy could never accept such a position.

The other possibility is that God is enclosed in man. This needs to be paraphrased. To say that there is no God outside of man but that there is that in man which may be called God, is the equivalent of saying that there is no God, but that there is something in man which we may consider valuable or good for whatever reason. Therefore, if we do not wish to use the word "God" just as a name for what is valuable or good, we may take this second possibility to mean, not that God is

---

[2] *The Life of Tolstoy*, Vol. II, Ch. II, p. 58.
[3] *Tolstoy or Dostoevsky: An Essay in Contrast*, Ch. 4, iii, p. 265.

enclosed in man, but that He is both in man and outside of him. Dr Steiner's comments are made with reference to a quotation from Tolstoy:

> I felt God clearly for the first time; that He existed and that I existed in Him; that the only thing that existed was I in Him: in Him like a limited thing in an unlimited thing, in Him also like a limited being in which He existed.

To interpret this in terms of the essay *On Life* we should say that the "I" is reasonable consciousness or the real self, not the animal personality; otherwise the words, "the only thing that existed was I in Him", would not occur. To interpret it in terms of *What I Believe*, vii and viii, and *The Kingdom of God is Within You*, iv, we should call the "I" the son of God. But it is asserted that reasonable consciousness or the self is beyond time and space, in which case it cannot be "limited". For the same reason the son of God cannot be limited either, so that it is hard to see what Tolstoy's distinction is between the self and God, or between the son of God and the Father. Indeed he says:

> The Christian teaching brings man back to the elementary consciousness of himself: not of himself as an animal but of himself as God—the divine spark of himself, a son of God of the same nature as the Father but confined in an animal husk.

And it appears that the son of God in man merges with the Father in proportion as it frees itself from man's animal nature. To use the mathematical analogy, the Father is like infinity, like an infinite continuation of the son of God, which is itself unlimited. If we regard reasonable consciousness or the self in *On Life* as being the son of God, there is no concept in that essay which we can identify with the Father; the son is also the Father.

3 *The Self, Consciousness, and Love*

In *On Life* the word "God" is not used except in quotations, and that essay is undoubtedly Tolstoy's most systematic attempt to expound a metaphysic. If we want to scrutinise Tolstoyan metaphysics, we must chiefly consider *On Life*, where he apparently tries not to make statements on matters that cannot be verified, or are not self-evident, but where, of course, he assumes far more to be self-evident than what is in fact so. The influence of Schopenhauer is apparent in many places in the essay. Tolstoy is indebted to him for the definition of life, the distinction between observation and knowledge, and the distinction between spatio-temporal manifestations and the realm beyond time and space—though the latter distinction assumes a peculiar form in Tolstoy's thought. But Schopenhauer had little to tell him about the misery of life, or about asceticism or love, which he did not himself "prove on the pulses". It was some terrible, personal experience—"the Arzamas misery"—that brought Tolstoy to despair, and his asceticism and self-devotion were consequences of this. In working out his salvation, he had sufficient guidance in the Christian tradition without needing to turn to Schopenhauer. When Levin in his despair read Schopenhauer, substituting "love" for "will", he was consoled, but not for more than two days. The resemblance between Tolstoy's and Schopenhauer's doctrines of love, and the similarity between the asceticism of the two men, with its praise of chastity and voluntary poverty, are at least as much due to the common elements in Indian and primitive Christian thought, as to the fact that Tolstoy made a study of Schopenhauer's works.

Tolstoy asserted that for all men the good of animal existence is equal to zero, and remains zero whatever it may be multiplied by; Schopenhauer, that evil is positive and good negative—pleasure and happiness being "only the good hours of an ague".[4] Both writers expressed the view that no satisfaction of desire provides the pleasure that was expected, because either satisfaction is followed by weariness and satiety or the craving continues. Tolstoy's description of the egoistic pursuit of well-being and its inevitable defeat, in Chapter 1 of *On Life*, "The fundamental contradiction of human life", recalls Schopenhauer's account of how everyone subject to the *principium individuationis* desires everything for himself, and of how, although the "knowing subject" cannot as such be

---

[4] Webster. Tolstoy, *On Life*, xxvi. Schopenhauer, *Parerga and Paralipomena,* Vol. II, 1851, Ch. XII, "*Nachträge zur Lehre vom Leiden der Welt*", sec. 149.

G

identified with the consciousness of any particular individual, yet every individual tends to make itself the centre of the world, as if all the rest of nature existed only in idea, with the result that there is conflict of the will with itself and war of all against all.[5]

Relevant too is Schopenhauer's comparison of men with animals. He says that man's happiness and misery have the same material basis as animals', which is the presence or else the absence of health, food, shelter, and the opportunity for sexual satisfaction. But man suffers more than animals because he is more sensitive and more passionate, and has the powers of reflection, memory, and foresight. To increase his pleasures he increases his needs; he worries about ambition and honour, and pursues mental pleasures, to overcome boredom: "need and boredom are the two poles of human life". And a man is further tormented by passionate love obstinately directed towards one person. Moreover, death is something very real to man, who can contemplate it, whereas animals fly from it instinctively without really knowing what it is.[6]

A similar view of human life underlies Tolstoy's distinction between animal personality and reasonable consciousness. For the latter is outside time and space, so that all that a man has within time and space is animal personality: all those aspirations that belong to the personalities of men, and that are not found among animals, are in theory denied. For Schopenhauer such aspirations increase the measure of suffering in human life out of all proportion to its pleasures, so that it is desirable, as Sir Isaiah Berlin puts it, to reduce "human vulnerability by reducing man himself to the condition of the utmost quietism, where, being passionless, he cannot be frustrated or humiliated or wounded".[7] For Tolstoy such aspirations are simply not recognised:

> The needs of the animal personality can always be satisfied. Man has not the right to say: What shall I eat? How shall I

---

[5] *The World as Will and Idea*, Book IV, sec. 61. See P. Gardiner, *Schopenhauer*, Ch. VI, p. 265.

[6] *Parerga*, Vol. II, Ch. XII, sec. 153, translated in a volume with the misleading title *The Essential Schopenhauer*, pp. 88-90. London (Unwin Books), 1962.

[7] *The Hedgehog and the Fox*. IV, p. 73.

be clothed? If he lives a rational life all his needs are satisfied as are those of a bird or a flower.[8]

And he argues that man should have no fear of death, because he consists of (1) matter, which is indestructible, (2) animal consciousness (and the animal perpetuates itself in the species), and (3) reasonable consciousness, which is immortal.[9] Reasonable consciousness is beyond time and space, and is the same for us all; the only important difference between people lies in the varying degrees to which their animal personalities are subject to it. Refined human needs, ambition, honour, the pleasures of the mind, and passionate human love, do not matter. We have seen already that what is usually understood by love Tolstoy dismisses as preference based on personal interest. But reflection, memory, and foresight do matter, because they are associated with reason, which poisons personal life: the more we reflect and contemplate death, the more certain do we become that the animal personality must be subjected to reason, and its needs reduced to a minimum.

The distinction between animal consciousness and reasonable consciousness is essential to Tolstoy's system. He says that it would seem that the self is consciousness, but, as a man's consciousness at a given moment will pass, his real self cannot be identified with his transitory consciousnesses, but is, rather, that which unites the whole series of consecutive, transitory consciousnesses into one. When he falls asleep, the series is interrupted and there is a cessation of consciousness in time, but when he wakes up he is still the same self. Yet what is this self? We are told that the answer lies in the simple words of a child: "I like this . . . I don't like that". The real self is that which for no observable reason likes one thing and not another, and is called character. It is flatly denied that character is the result of heredity and environment, and asserted that an individual already has a definite capacity for loving

[8] *On Life*, xxi. Tolstoy never acknowledged a problem of overpopulation, attributing the famines in Russia to human wickedness. It is wrong to take food from another, according to him, and wrong to eat food that another needs for his own survival. But if a man is being starved to death by a wicked government, he should consent to die, as he should consent to death however it comes (*On Life*, xxxiii).

[9] *Ibid.*, xxxii.

one thing and not loving another "when he enters the world"—
which is a theory like Schopenhauer's; only Schopenhauer
admitted that such a theory leads to a difficult problem.
According to him, character is innate and sprung from the
same eternity as the will, which is beyond time, and therefore character does not admit of any but a transcendental explanation. But if the will, as the thing-in-itself, is identical in all
its manifestations, how is it that there is qualitative, ethical
diversity between characters? [10]

In Tolstoy it is reasonable consciousness which is eternal,
and the animal personality is in time and space, so that there
may be endless diversity between various animal personalities,
even though ethical difference is taken to depend only on the
degree of subjection to reason. But Tolstoy asserts that, though
the personality is in time and space, character is not. How,
then, can there be diversity between characters? We are told
that there is this diversity, or that men's inner selves, their
capacities for liking one thing and not another, present sharp
contrasts; and yet we are also, apparently, to assume that this
self, this ego or life that a man is conscious of, is reasonable
consciousness, which, like the Logos of St John, is the beginning
of everything (*"nachalo . . . v nëm vsë i ot nego vsë"*), and in
which a man

> does not even see any parentage, but recognizes his oneness,
> beyond time and space, with other reasonable consciousnesses
> so that they enter into him and he into them. [11]

It would seem that, if one man's self is beyond time and
space, it cannot be divided off from other such selves, but must
be one with them. That being so, everyone's self, as distinct
from his personality, is the same, and one man's likes and
dislikes cannot be equated with his self, but must be due to his
personality, since they differ from another's.

The arguments Tolstoy uses to support his theory about the
self are so sophistical that one wonders how he can have formulated them. He argues that, although in sleep there is the
same cessation of consciousness in time as there is in death, a

[10] *Neue Paralipomena*, Ch. vii, *"Zur Ethik"*, sec. 248; see *The Essential Schopenhauer*, pp. 160-1.
[11] *On Life*, vii, x, xii, xxviii and xxix.

man is not afraid to fall asleep, not because he believes he will shortly wake up again (he may not), but because he knows that his real self is outside time. Another argument consists in saying that the changes which take place in the substance of a body, and the changes of consciousness in time, are so great that, were it not for an unchanging self outside time and space, the organism, body and temporal consciousness, would, as it were, fall to pieces, for there would be nothing to give it unity or identity.

But animals too would have to have such a real and actual self to give unity and identity to their organisms and unite their consciousnesses. Indeed, the argument about likes and dislikes is extended to them, so that it is hard to see what is meant by "animal consciousness". If animal consciousness is an animal's real and actual self, and if that self is outside time and space, then, as animal consciousness is not the same as reasonable consciousness, there should be some obscure distinction between reasonable consciousness and the self, which is not explained in the essay. If, however, the term "animal consciousness" is used only to indicate the series of consciousnesses in time, we still have to explain how it is that a dog does not fall apart when it goes to sleep.

In Appendix I to *On Life* the definition of life as a "striving after good" is applied to animals as well as men. An animal is conscious of that striving, and therein resides its self; and what an animal strives for is its own good and that of its whelps or herd. But if a man strives for personal, family, or social well-being, he is said not to live:

> We only recognize life as being present in our fellows or in ourselves when our animal personality is subject not only to the laws of the organism but also to the higher law of reasonable consciousness.[12]

It has to be shown that, in spite of the definition of life that is given, an animal life is for man not life. This is necessary to Tolstoy for two purposes. One is to establish a theory of immortality. These arguments serve as the basis for a powerful outpouring in Chapter xxxi to the effect that the self of his dead brother continues to live in him. The other purpose is to

[12] *Ibid.*, xiv.

find an ethic, by virtue of which any way of life that does not involve self-renunciation and spiritual love may be condemned. It has to be shown that there are grounds for denouncing the man who is living for himself or for his family or nation.

Man is egoistic, with the result that there is appalling conflict. Reasonable consciousness shows man this, together with all the other certain miseries of existence, the unattainability of individual happiness, and the certainty of death; and man is reduced to despair. This egoistic existence is animal life, or not life at all; and human life must have not only some other aim, but also a different source. For a man can hardly subdue his animal personality, or sacrifice his own pleasures to alleviate the sufferings of foreigners or strangers, if there is not something in him other than animal personality and animal consciousness. Tolstoy sees man as made up of two entities, one egoistic and the other loving.

The theory that in reasonable consciousness man recognises his oneness, beyond time and space, with other reasonable consciousnesses, is similar to Schopenhauer's theory of sympathy. Schopenhauer held that, the will being identical in all its manifestations, the true basis of morality is expressed in the Sanskrit formula, "That art thou" ("*Tat tvam asi*"): if a man does not regard others empirically as individuals, but recognises that his inmost being subsists in every living thing, he will discover in this truth the source of all loving-kindness ("*agape*"). A compassionate man becomes so identified with another that he as directly desires to reduce the other's suffering as he would his own. Indeed, this identification is described in *Master and Man*. But according to Schopenhauer, character is constant; the proportion of egoism to compassion in a man cannot change. For an egoistic man, none but egoistic motives have any appreciable effect.[13] Even if, then, he came to see the vanity of the pursuit of personal well-being, he would remain incapable of performing acts of disinterested virtue, and his state of mind might be that expressed by Tolstoy in these words:

[13] *On the Foundation of Morality*, secs. 16, 18, 20, and 22, translated by A. B. Bullock. London (Sonnenschein), 1903.

It would be possible to live for reasonable consciousness, but it is not worth while and I do not want to. Serve that source from whence I came—God? Why? If God exists, he will find people to serve him without me. And why should I do it? One can contemplate this play of life as long as one does not find it dull, and when it is dull one can go away and kill one-self.[14]

But Tolstoy affirms that the real, inalienable good of love is always within reach here and now. Love is in the self, and is a motive capable of compelling one to live for reasonable consciousness. It is activity on the only path left open by reason.

The relation of love to the self, however, presents a difficulty, for Tolstoy appears to make two incompatible assertions. He says that the self is that which likes one thing and not another; and he says that human life is an incessant movement, involving a greater and greater subjection of the personality to reason and the manifestation of a greater degree of love. The man who understands life

> knows that this love of one thing and hatred (*nelyubov'*, dislike) of another that he brought with him into this present existence is the very essence of his life, that it is not merely an accidental feature, but that it alone has the movement of life—and he places his life entirely in this movement, in this increase of love.[15]

If dislike originated in the personality, we could understand that it might be diminished as the personality is submitted to reason. As it is, we are told that the movement of life entails an alteration in the character. How that which is beyond time and space can be subject to change, is not indicated. The movement that Tolstoy can be most intelligibly held to be speaking of consists in a gradual subdual of the animal personality; but we want to know how such a change can have any effect on the self or character. Tolstoy wishes to accept a part of Schopenhauer's theory of character, in order to support his own theory of the self, but he rejects the corollary that character is constant.

Further confusion arises when it is declared that human life begins only with the appearance of a reasonable consciousness.

[14] *On Life*, xxii.   [15] *Ibid.*, xxx.

Tolstoy's arguments that a man's self is outside time and space are either not valid, or else they show that the self of an animal is also outside time and space, even though animals are egoistic. Man's self or character, we learn, is capable of dislike; but in reasonable consciousness all men in whom reasonable consciousness has awakened, are united. Reasonable consciousness is both eternal, like the self, and capable of awakening in time. Again we meet the implication that reasonable consciousness and the self are distinct, even though they both constitute the essence of man's life.

The thesis of *On Life*, though it is advanced as a rational philosophy, is an ill-fitting dress for mystical dogmatism. It is so muddled and obscure that it is not surprising that it has been largely disregarded, though some people of a theistic or theosophic inclination have praised it. The essay exemplifies the general truth about Tolstoy that, while his destructive criticism is very good, his positive theories are attempts at self-deception. He needed a renunciatory ethic: by speaking of the awakening of reasonable consciousness—obviously feeling that in his own case it had begun to stir with "the Arzamas misery"—he was able to condemn those years of his life when he had not attempted self-renunciation; and by maintaining that reasonable consciousness is outside space and time, he could have that in the name of which renunciation might be made, and through which he might attain the immortality for which he longed. Moreover, he knew "the spiritual delight of love" and regarded this as the best, and in some moments the only good, part of himself. With the metaphysical system he had worked out, he had little difficulty in attributing this power of love to the immortal part of man, so that he could believe it would increase in proportion as the animal personality is subjected to reason.

4 *The External World*

Lyubov Axelrod's interpretation of Tolstoy's metaphysics is as follows.[16] God, in the essay *On Life*, is absolute, endless world reason; and reason is the inner essence of all external

[16] "Tolstoy's Inner Tragedy as the Basis of his Doctrine", x, *O Tolstom*, ed. V. M. Friche.

things, of which some are its reflection, and others a reflection of a reflection. This ultra-idealistic conception precludes recognition of a personal God outside the world; according to it, God and the world are identical, so that it can be regarded as a kind of pantheism. But Tolstoy could not hold this theory consistently because it did not answer his chief question, What meaning has my life? which, as we have seen, represents the search for an aim. The aim of life, as it is expressed in the *Confession*, includes a morally-obligatory relation of man to an absolute principle. The question is, then: What attributes should be peculiar to this absolute principle, by virtue of which earthly life may be understood to have an aim? The *Confession* answers this question quite clearly, says Axelrod referring, presumably, to the idea there of the will of God. But, she says, let us look at the Tolstoyan formulation of the basis of religion:

> Religion is the definition of man's relation to the Source of all things and of man's purpose in life which follows from that relation, and it supplies rules of conduct resulting from that purpose . . . And this purpose involves practical demands on man in accord with the rule, Do to others as you wish them to do to you.[17]

One asks what the connexion is between man's relation to the Source of all and the Golden Rule. According to Tolstoyan pantheism, man is both a part of the universal reason or absolute consciousness, and also animal personality, that is, a part of the sensible world which is mere appearance; thus, like every creature, he is related to the Source of all as a part to the whole. And it is obvious that in such a system moral rules of conduct can have no foundation; the pantheistic world-view cannot in itself supply such a foundation: *sub specie aeternitatis* "everything is permitted". Therefore, in order to establish an ethic, Tolstoy was compelled after all to acknowledge a personal God, Creator, Lawgiver and Appointer of aims.

Something can be said for this interpretation of Axelrod's, but it is not entirely correct. In the first place, one can only in the vaguest sense call Tolstoy a pantheist. Schopenhauer pointed out that to identify the world with God is to say nothing

[17] *What is Religion?*, xiv.

at all.[18]   At most, pantheists, in asserting that the inner nature of the world is God, are making a distinction between its inner nature and its outer nature, and hence, perhaps, implying a kind of dualism.   The question is, therefore, whether Axelrod was right in saying that according to Tolstoy external things are only a reflection of the inner essence.

Certainly there is evidence in *On Life* for saying that she was.   "Reasonable life exists.   It is the only thing that does exist", we find in Chapter xiv, where, too, he speaks of the unreality ("*prizrachnost'* ") of man's animal existence; and in Chapter xxvii it is said that everything that is limited by time and space is a phantom.

But *On Life* is an ethical, as well as a metaphysical, work, and the doctrine of using the animal personality as an instrument subordinate to reason would be meaningless if that instrument were a phantom.   The essay makes more sense if we regard the remarks about the unreality of the sensible world as exceptional and semi-rhetorical, and if we take the view that Tolstoy acknowledged the actual existence in themselves in time and space of things in the external, sensible world.   Indeed, there is good evidence for taking such a view in Chapters xi, xii, and xiii.

These chapters are a refutation of those theories which consist in regarding man as an object of observation, overlooking what are called his psychic phenomena, as they are too complex, and attempting to understand human life by means of a study of animals, plants, and matter.   Tolstoy argues that such theories have everything in a false perspective: they imply that good and reasonable consciousness are unknowable, but that man as an animal is knowable, that animals and plants are more knowable, and that matter is the most knowable of all—whereas in fact the reverse is the case.   This is the distinction between knowledge and observation: man fully knows only what he is conscious of in himself—the law of reason and the good after which he strives—and he also knows his own animal personality when it is subject to reason;   other men he knows, too, to the extent to which their lives accord with the same law as his

[18] *Parerga*, Vol. ii, Ch. v, "*Einige Worte über den Pantheismus*", sec. 69. See Gardiner, *Schopenhauer*, Ch. iii, p. 72.

own, but animals he hardly knows at all, and he can only observe plants and matter.

> The more observable the manifestation of the object in space and time the less comprehensible is it to us,

and:

> We cannot get to know ourselves from the laws that govern animals, though we know animals only from the law we know in ourselves.

It is in Chapter XIII that the two sentences occur to which Axelrod chiefly refers in support of her case that Tolstoy is what she calls a pantheist. But it seems she has misunderstood them. They are:

> The animal kingdom is for us only a reflection of what we know in ourselves. The material world is, as it were, the reflection of a reflection.

Their meaning should be obvious from their context. Indeed, a few paragraphs further on it is said that the body and the matter constituting man exist of themselves, and they are the instrument and material for the work of true life.

This destroys the basis of Axelrod's argument that strict analysis of Tolstoy's metaphysical system reveals that according to it everything is permitted. But one could devise an argument similar to hers, as follows: As reasonable consciousness is eternal, beyond time and space, and present in each of us, we are already inwardly united with one another and shall remain thus united, however much our animal personalities may struggle against one another; one animal personality may therefore tear another apart: we love in the spirit; in the body everything is permitted.

However, besides asserting that reasonable consciousness is eternal, and that man has a capacity for spiritual love in his self, Tolstoy also attempts to prove that the good of the animal personality is illusory, so that only folly and ignorance would make us think that any advantage was to be gained by material struggle or murder.

Renunciation of the welfare of animal personality is a law of human life. If it is not accomplished freely, expressing itself in submission to reasonable consciousness, it is accomplished forcibly in each man at the bodily death of his animal personality, when under the weight of his sufferings he desires only one thing: to be freed from the painful consciousness of his perishing personality and pass over to another plane of existence.[19]

Therefore the doctrine of the awakening of reasonable consciousness in a man is essential to this system, since many might prefer to wait till death before renouncing the welfare of animal personality. The sooner and the more fully reasonable consciousness, with its negation of personal good, awakens in a man, the better it is for everybody else—except his wife and children.

5 The Law of Reason

The term "law of reason" has a prominent place in *On Life*, though its meaning is vague. In Chapter x we find this:

Reason for man is the law by which his life is accomplished, just such a law as that for the animal by which it feeds itself and multiplies; as the law for the plant by which grass and trees blossom and bear fruit; as the law of the heavenly bodies by which the earth and the planets move.

There is only this difference:

In the external world we see this subordination to the law of reason, but in ourselves we recognize this law as that which we ought ourselves to fulfil.
. . . Our life consists in the accomplishment of this law, in subjecting our animal personality to the law of reason for the attainment of good.

But the difference between scientific and moral laws is, of course, enormous. A moral law implies choice; in this particular case we have a choice between subjecting our personalities to reason in youth and waiting till old age and the approach of death, or waiting for some disaster or period of

[19] *On Life*, xvi.

despair in our lives, before we make the necessary renunciation. It is arguable that the "ought" of the moral law is derived from the proposition that the good of animal existence is equal to zero: we ought to submit our animal personalities to reason in order to obtain true life beyond space and time, for to reject true life is to choose misery. But this is to make a hypothetical imperative the essence of Tolstoy's ethics; Kant's hypothetical imperative tells you what to do if you wish to achieve a certain end. In this case the end is deliverance of the personality from suffering. Of course, the personality will in any case continue to suffer until it is destroyed; but, if it is not submitted to reason, its sufferings, being unexplained by the subject, merely evoke in him "an ever-increasing despair and exasperation that can never be pacified". We can, by our attitude to it, increase our own suffering to infinity; but we can also reduce it to minute proportions, Tolstoy says, by resignation achieved through submission to reason.[20]

Though this is possibly a true explanation of the motive that impelled Tolstoy along a path of renunciation in his later years, he nevertheless rejected it in theory. Buddhism, in so far as it is based on the assumption that a self-sufficient personality should deliver itself from suffering, he called "negative paganism", positive paganism being the belief that a man has a right to individual happiness.[21]

Alternatively we may take Tolstoy to mean that, apart from the question of the possibility or the impossibility of personal happiness, the law of reason simply requires us to submit the animal personality to it, thereby making a series of acts of renunciation, and releasing the love that is in us. This requirement is like the categorical imperative, addressed to us as moral beings; in which case the attempt to demonstrate that the good of animal existence is equal to zero, is quite unnecessary. The law of reason we recognise in ourselves in so far as we are God, and it is another name for the will of God. We, as God, require ourselves to renounce the welfare of the personality and do whatever we are urged to do by the love which is thus released.

[20] *Ibid.*, xxxiv and xxxv.
[21] A footnote to *Religion and Morality*.

6 The Will of God

Tolstoy's creed appears in the famous *Reply to the Synod's Edict of Excommunication.* It is as follows:

> I believe in this: I believe in God, whom I understand as Spirit, as Love, as the Source of all. I believe that he is in me and I in him. I believe that the will of God is most clearly and intelligibly expressed in the teaching of the man Jesus, whom to consider as God and pray to, I esteem the greatest blasphemy. I believe that man's true welfare lies in fulfilling God's will, and his will is that men should love one another and should consequently do to others as they wish others to do to them— of which it is said in the Gospels that in this is the law and the prophets. I believe therefore that the meaning of the life of every man is to be found only in increasing the love that is in him; that this increase of love leads man, even in this life, to ever greater and greater blessedness, and after death gives him the more blessedness the more love he has, and helps more than anything else towards the establishment of the Kingdom of God on earth: that is, to the establishment of an order of life in which the discord, deception, and violence that now rule will be replaced by free accord, by truth, and by the brotherly love of one for another. I believe that to obtain progress in love there is only one means: prayer—not public in churches, plainly forbidden by Jesus, but private prayer, like the sample given us by Jesus, consisting of the renewing and strengthening in our own consciousness of the meaning of our life and of our complete dependence on the will of God.

Most of this is consistent with the essay *On Life*, but there are a few difficulties. One, which is presented by the phrase "the Kingdom of God on earth", will be discussed later. Another lies in the question: If God (or reason) is Spirit, how is He also the Source ("*nachalo*") of all? Though he did not press the point, Tolstoy seems to have accepted the First Cause argument for the existence of God. In a private letter he wrote:

> I was born of my mother, and she of my grandmother, and she of my great-grandmother, but the very first—of whom? And I inevitably arrive at God.[22]

[22] Quoted by Aylmer Maude in "Thoughts Selected from Private Letters" in Tolstoy's *Recollections and Essays*.

The First Cause argument is brought out also in *Confession*, xii. Evidently the trouble with it is that it has an insufficient relation to Tolstoy's spiritual striving: to believe that God created the physical world will not in itself lead to salvation; He must be experienced inwardly in the present. But a question Tolstoy never attempts to answer is this: If God is Spirit, and if things in the external world actually exist in themselves, what power did He have to create those things? How did matter come from Spirit? And if Axelrod is right in saying that, according to Tolstoy, external things are only a reflection of an inner essence which is reason or God, questions arise as to how and why the reflection has the form that it has.

In this connexion it is remarkable that Tolstoy recommended a book *Esquisses de Philosophie Critique*, containing a statement of A. Spir's conclusions, which are in the tradition of Kant, and that the following is a characteristic passage approved of by Tolstoy:

> The perception that God is neither the cause nor in any sense a sufficient reason for the existence of the world, and cannot be used to explain it, establishes the independence of physical science *vis-à-vis* of morality and religion. The perception that the physical world is abnormal, founded on a delusion, and that physical science has only a relative truth, establishes the independence and the primacy of morality and of religion *vis-à-vis* of physical science.[23]

In view of this it might seem that Tolstoy had no reason to assert that God is the Source of all, or that reasonable consciousness is the Logos in the sense of the beginning of everything. But he had a reason. For if God is not the cause of the existence of the physical world, or if that world is founded on a delusion, it follows that, once you grant that the good of animal existence is equal to zero, you may as well commit suicide whether you believe in God or not; for you cannot regard your personality as an instrument intended by God to be used in the work of life, if you think that God did not give you it: you may destroy your own animal personality, while contuining to love other people in the spirit. Therefore, simply so as not to commit

---

[23] Quoted by Aylmer Maude in his introduction to his translation of *On Life* etc.

suicide, Tolstoy had to say that the existence he was about to end was given him for a purpose. To do this, he had to maintain that this God he had found within himself is, in some sense, a Creator and also had some intention in causing the existence of the physical world, that is to say, has a will.

Hence follow the assumption that God indeed had the power to create the physical world, and a dogmatic answer to the question what His intention was in doing so. But as Tolstoy's is a life-denying ethic, the answer is unsatisfactory. In the first place, it only refers to the human race and to what is necessary for human existence; and, secondly, it is, in effect, that God created men in order that they may attain unity; but, as it is only the animal personality that is holding them apart, the existence of the animal personality is, ultimately, not justified. This point will be discussed in the next chapter. The point to be noted here is that, because he believed that the good of animal existence is equal to zero, Tolstoy had to believe in the will of God if only to establish that suicide is wrong.

A third difficulty in his creed lies in the statement that the will of God is that men should love one another, and consequently observe the Golden Rule. In *The Kingdom of God is Within You*, IV, it is said that a Christian recognises life not in his own personality, and not in an association of personalities, but in God.

> And to do the will of God he sacrifices his personality and domestic and social welfare. The motive of his life is love.

Love for whom? For God? We know that according to Tolstoy love for God is possible only because God, or the son of God who is of the same nature as the Father, is already in man; so that this doctrine means, as Axelrod expresses it, that a part of the divinity in man loves God, or, in other words, love for God is God's love for Himself.[24] If, on the other hand, the motive of a Christian's life is love for other human beings and for animals, the conclusion is the same. Clearly, from Tolstoy's point of view, it is a gross error to love the personalities of others; one can only love the divinity in them, recognising one's unity with their reasonable consciousness; so that love

[24] "Tolstoy's Inner Tragedy", XI.

for others is God's love for Himself (and if animals have no reasonable consciousness, one cannot love them at all). Therefore this particular tenet about the will of God amounts to this: The will of God is that we, as God, should love God and consequently observe the Golden Rule; and love for God causes us to do the will of God. This is only to say that observance of the Golden Rule is a consequence of love for God; in which case the concept of the will of God can be dispensed with in this context. Indeed, it is said later in *The Kingdom of God is Within You*, IV, that the commandment of love is not a commandment in the strict sense of the word, but the expression of the very essence of the Christian teaching.

Tolstoy was aware of such difficulties when he wrote in his diary:

> People speak of the will of God, in the sense of God's aim. God cannot have any aim. For Him everything is attained. So that the motive of his [a true believer's?] activity can be only one: love.[25]

Tolstoy, as has often been observed, was forever tormentedly seeking God, and the speculation in his later diaries as to the nature of God is part of that search. Nicolas Weisbein in the last pages of *L'Evolution Religieuse de Tolstoi* considers the idea of God which is expressed in these later diaries, and Tolstoy's final meditations on the nature of faith. These private reflections, however, do not concern us here, since this is a study of the writer's public philosophy. In Chapter XIV of *What is Religion?* he is able to enunciate the principles of the "true", universal, Tolstoyan religion without speaking of the will of God: in man there dwells a part of the Divine Origin (*"nachalo"*) of all, and man can increase this divine element by suppressing his passions and increasing love in himself.

However, in the last chapter of *What is Religion?* the phrases "to serve God" and "to fulfil the will of God" occur as if they were unavoidable in Tolstoy's moralising. Axelrod is right, though probably for the wrong reason, in her assertion that Tolstoy felt compelled to acknowledge a personal God, Who is

[25] 10 Augus 1904.

H

Creator, Lawgiver and Appointer of aims. He had a tendency, which is evident, for example, in *Master and Man* and *Resurrection*, to think of God as Master (*"khozyain"*). The statement on the last page of *Resurrection*, that we were sent here by someone's will and for some purpose, is an echo of the statement in *Confession*, xii, that God is that Will which produced each man and desires something of him, and a repetition of the premise behind the discourse of *Religion and Morality*, that the meaning of life lies solely in serving that Will which has produced man and the entire universe not for man's aims but for its own.

We read in the same paragraph in *Resurrection* that the Master's will is expressed in the five commandments of the Sermon on the Mount. These, then, it may be said, are divine commands which are dictated to us by a superior power. But let us consider them, as Tolstoy understood them: "Do not be angry, do not lust, do not take oaths, do not go to law, do not fight." They are all derived from the same two beliefs: that we need to renounce the welfare of the personality, and that love is the immortal part of man. Anger is, of course, a violation of spiritual love; and to take an oath is to bind oneself to a king or an organisation, thereby destroying one's freedom of conscience, and permitting oneself in advance to do things, in the name of king, country or state, which one would not do if one regarded oneself as individually responsible. The fourth and fifth commandments are included in the ideal of non-resistance to evil, which is discussed together with the ideal of complete celibacy in the next chapter. But it should be clear already that, without a belief in the possibility of individual happiness, these five commandments cannot reasonably be broken; only if we thought that it was worth striving to obtain or maintain personal, domestic, or social well-being, should we find it necessary to justify anger, seek sexual satisfaction, take oaths, go to law, or fight. It is evident that observance of the five commandments, like observance of the Golden Rule, is a consequence of love for God, as Tolstoy understands that love; so that the concept of the Master's will is not essential to these five commandments, and one need not speak of "commandments" at all: if a man loves God, he will not be angry, and will not lust, take oaths, go to law, or fight, in so far as his feelings and actions are consistent with his love.

But it may be said that God has will in that we are He and we have to make an effort to keep the so-called commandments. To submit our personalities to the law of reason requires effort presumably; we are probably to suppose that this effort is *motivated* by love, which resides in the self, though it is not clear whether it is *made* by the self or the personality. Further discussion of this point is precluded by the obscurities of Tolstoy's system. Although it is in fact not possible to regard the self and reasonable consciousness as one and the same, yet because Tolstoy seems to identify them, argument reaches the point of saying that, quite apart from the effort involved, in our accepting the need to submit the personality to reason, God is obeying Himself.

IV

Suicide and Sacrifice

1 Non-Resistance and Celibacy

Tolstoy's ideals of non-resistance to evil by violence and of complete abstention from sexual relations are both derived from the same two beliefs, one of which is positive—that love is the essence of man's soul—and the other negative—that we need to renounce the welfare of the personality. He himself had already renounced the welfare of his personality before he came to believe in God—he was going to kill himself—and this fact is fundamental to his understanding of Christianity and his formulation of an ethical code. For this code, when expressed in a concrete form applicable to life, is negative; the five commandments of the Sermon on the Mount, which for him constitute the essence of Christ's teaching, he interprets negatively. For a man who recognises the impossibility of individual happiness, knowing that the pursuit of it would merely cause further suffering to himself and others, and who believes that consequently it is senseless to strive for domestic or social well-being, it is illogical to break these commandments.

Tolstoy's choice, at the time of his conversion, was between suicide and a life of self-sacrifice. Nothing else was possible; he could not go on living as before. Either there is no God, and life is a cheat; or there is a God, and life takes its meaning from its divine origin. If the latter is true, it is inconceivable that God should grant individuals life for their own enjoyment, since that enjoyment is unattainable and the desire for it results in despair, from which the individual can only be rescued by the substitution of some other end. Since life in time and space derives its significance solely through its dependence on God, Who is beyond time and space, any activity is meaningless if it is not in accordance with the will of God, and the only end to which the individual can dedicate his life without a return to despair is service of God, which necessarily involves self-sacrifice.

It is death, above all, says Tolstoy, that proves the vanity of the personal life in the sense of "worldly, personal life" ("*mirskaya, lichnaya zhizn'* "), "isolated (*odinokaya*) personal life", or "life for oneself"; but true life ("*zhizn' istinnaya*"), if one participates in it by foregoing one's own will (personal desires) and doing the will of the Father, lifts one beyond the death that destroys the personality, since it is the common life of humanity bound up with past, present, and future.[1] It follows, then, that true life is a life of love. Besides the "corporeal personal life" ("*plotskaya lichnaya zhizn'* "), "which proceeds from a male parent in the womb of his physical mother", each man has that in him which is free and is born of God, and which he should exalt in himself to attain true life. If a man merges his life into God's, he becomes united with others; he finds life in the son of man, which is the son of God and is present in us all.[2] Tolstoy is opposed to individualism, and therefore he rejects the theory of personal immortality, as is clear from *What I Believe*. As for his own theory of the immortality of the self in *On Life*, nothing definite emerges from it that could not be inferred from *What I Believe*: the personality is mortal, but in reasonable consciousness man can participate in everlasting life.

Tolstoy insists strenuously that the doctrine that force should never be used to resist evil is the key to Christ's teaching, and that it cannot be modified without impairing the essence of that teaching, because to him non-resistance is a form of self-sacrifice. I should not renounce my animal personality, he says, but only its welfare; that personality I should submit to the demands of reasonable consciousness and use as an instrument for promoting the good of others. But if my own personal welfare is vain to me, another man's is vain to him, and I am doing him a disservice in promoting it. I can, logically, only benefit another by persuading him that his suffering has its origin in an erroneous valuation of personality, and that he should regard his body merely as a tool of the spirit.[3] But if

[1] *What I Believe*, viii.   [2] *Ibid.*, vii.   [3] *On Life*, xxxv and xvi.

he asks me what he should then do with that tool, I am lost for an answer. This point has been made by L. I. Axelrod, who said:

> It is clear, therefore, that to love one's neighbour means, from this point of view, to love his spiritual being, i.e. to feel a tie with his "reasonable absolute ego". But one must maintain complete indifference towards his concrete empirical aspirations. For, since I regard my own temporal and spatial personality as illusory and insignificant, and all its aspirations as a cruel chimera and the greatest calamity, which forms a powerful obstacle in the path to real life and the highest happiness, then I should naturally look upon my neighbour's concrete personality in exactly the same way.[4]

It is important to distinguish between the meanings of "personal life" and "animal personality". "Personal life" is described in *On Life* as "the life in which it is necessary that all should love me alone and I love only myself, and in which I want to get as much enjoyment as possible and free myself from suffering and death", and it is condemned as itself the greatest and most unceasing suffering.[5] It is the vain shadow of life which is called "isolated personal life" in *What I Believe*. "Animal personality", on the other hand, is a phrase used in *On Life* to indicate the organism or the sum of those attributes of a man that exist in time and space,[6] that is to say, all but his reasonable consciousness or real and special self. This is the "corporeal personal life" of *What I Believe*.

The isolated personal life is a negation of love, and, if the spirit of man is one, as is postulated, it may be arguable that it is sinful for men to live in mutual conflict. By renouncing one's personal life and acknowledging the spirit, one is united in spirit with humanity. Once this union is achieved, the value of the animal personality has yet to be demonstrated, but it is not necessarily denied.

But to regard the personality merely as a tool of the spirit

---

[4] "Tolstoy's Inner Tragedy as the Basis of his Doctrine", xi, *O Tolstom*, ed. V. M. Friche.

[5] *On Life*, xix. The phrase used here is "*zhizn' lichnosti*".

[6] *Ibid.*, xiii and xiv.

is to deny its value, as we have seen. For it is to imply that the earth is nothing but a shed full of tools; and that for a man to labour for the material well-being of others is like using a tool for the improvement of other tools, which are themselves useful only for the improvement of other tools, and so on to infinity. If tools have any value, it consists in the fact that their owners can use them to make their own lives more abundant. The owner of the body is the spirit; but, if the spirit is independent of the conditions of time and space, nothing that is done in time and space—no activity of the tools—can benefit or harm it. This is an argument not only for non-resistance to evil, which Tolstoy asserts, but also for inaction, which, illogically, he rejects. Once all the tools are perfected, which, to Tolstoy, can only mean, once everyone has decided that his personality is just a tool, they become utterly useless, and the human race should die out, as Pozdnyshev in *The Kreutzer Sonata* wants.[7]

If a man's real and actual self is beyond time and space, there is no reason why he should delight in his animal existence; on the contrary, it is a burden. But Tolstoy sees that it cannot be right that a man should simply get rid of that burden by suicide; he must have been given it for some purpose. Now the purpose of the individual, according to Tolstoy, is, as we have seen, to end his individuality by merging his life into God's; the merging occurs in spirit, and the body becomes a tool. A similar doctrine is applied to mankind. It is to be united in love, which means that all men will be at one with God and their bodies will become redundant. The argument that the body is a tool will then lose whatever validity it may have had, for there will be no more work, as the aim of life will have been achieved. There will then be nothing for it but to get rid of those bodies, not by slaughter, but by abstention from sexual relations. In other words, the species will commit suicide. Pozdnyshev's theory is not just Pozdnyshev's; it is not contradicted by Tolstoy in anything that was written after *The Kreutzer Sonata*, and not only is the statement of the ideal of complete celibacy or perfect chastity repeated in the *Afterword* to *The Kreutzer Sonata* and in *The Kingdom of God is Within You*, IV, but also the doctrine of general suicide by means of chastity

[7] *The Kreutzer Sonata*, XI.

is the logical outcome of the despairing passages of the *Con-fession*.

Chapter XI of the *Confession* is a chapter of self-condemna-tion, where Tolstoy singles out the badness of his own way of life as the prime cause of his despair:

> I understood that my question as to what my life is, and the answer—an evil—was quite correct. The only mistake was that the answer referred only to my life, while I had referred it to life in general. I asked myself what my life is, and got the reply: An evil and an absurdity. And really my life—a life of indulgence of desires—was senseless and evil, and there-fore the reply, 'Life is evil and an absurdity', referred only to my life, but not to human life in general.

By saying this, and by seeking solidarity with those who, in contrast with the people of his own parasitic class, labour to support life, he hoped to put an end to his despair. And indeed the despair disappears when life is believed to have an aim, and the suicidal desire to be rid of the body is replaced by an attitude of stoical indifference towards it. But the indifference is as general as the despair had once been. Seeing the cause of his despair over life in his individual worthlessness, Tolstoy sup-posed that everyone is worthless as an individual and only really alive as a manifestation of a divine, impersonal force.

The logic that binds *The Kreutzer Sonata* to the *Confession* could only have been broken if he had found some other mean-ing in the body than that it is a tool of the spirit. As it was, in renouncing his own personal welfare, he came to believe that all people should renounce the welfare of their personalities, meaning not just that each person should sacrifice himself for others, but that mankind as a whole should sacrifice itself. For when the individual's life is perfected, it ceases to exist in itself and is one with God and mankind; and when mankind is one, the idea of mutual service will be outmoded, the word "mutual" being meaningless within a unity, as it implies the existence of at least two entities. Then since the body, to Tolstoy, has no value in itself, it should be discarded, he says, when the time comes at which we can allow ourselves to believe that the spirit needs it no longer.

But if the spirit will not need the body at that uncertain

time in the future, logically it cannot need it now. Indeed, in *The Kingdom of God is Within You*, iv, we are told that life consists only in the freeing of the son of God existing in each man from the animal, and its approach to the Father—which means that life is fulfilled only in death. Since death, in Tolstoy's view, proves that the good of the animal personality is illusory, it cannot matter to him if one dies naturally or at the hands of an assassin. The only person who really suffers at a murder is the murderer, because he is in error. The victim is relieved of a burden which is a temptation, and of a tool which is evidently no longer wanted. If it were still wanted, it would not be destroyed:

> We are alive not because we safeguard ourselves, but because we are doing life's work.[8]

This is the only possible argument that can lie behind the following statement:

> All men are brothers equally. And if a Zulu comes to roast my children, the one thing I can do is to try to impress upon him that this is not advantageous and good for him; to impress this on him while submitting to his force—especially as there is no advantage for me in fighting him. Either he will overcome me and roast still more of my children, or I shall overcome him and my children will to-morrow fall ill and die with worse sufferings. It is inexpedient, because by submitting I certainly do better, while by resisting I do something doubtful.[9]

Tolstoy is not to be blamed for the suggestion that Zulus are cannibals, as he is only replying to a question which has been put to him: What would you do if a Zulu came to roast your children? The admiration that was felt for Tolstoy in his last years was largely due to the heroic way in which he stood out against the Tsarist government and attacked it in tremendous verbal onslaughts. His interpretation of Christ's teaching presented a high moral standpoint from which to condemn the

[8] *On Life*, xxxiii.

[9] A letter to M. A. Engelhardt, 1882, published with Aylmer Maude's translation of *What Then Must We Do?*; also included in the collection *Ripe Ears* (*Spelye kolos'ya*), compiled with Tolstoy's permission by D. R. Kudryavtsev, 1896; quoted by Plekhanov in "A Confusion of Ideas" ("*Smeshenie predstavleny*"), 1910, i, reprinted in *L. N. Tolstoy v russkoy kritike, Sbornik statey*, ed. S. P. Bychkov.

actions of the government. One wonders whether he could have expressed his beliefs to the cannibal equally eloquently.

God created men that they may attain unity; but it is only the animal personality that is keeping them apart; so the existence of the animal personality is not justified, and therefore we should never do anything doubtful in its defence. The person who by this reasoning adopts the principle of non-resistance to evil by violence is not actively sacrificing human lives for the sake of spiritual unity, but his conception of spiritual unity justifies him in not doing all he can to prevent the destruction of every value that we can ascribe to physical life and personality.

Hence it is that Tolstoyan non-resistance is the expression of an individual's desire to sacrifice himself transferred to mankind, the link that makes this transference possible being the belief in spiritual unity. The ideal of non-resistance flows from the same source as the ideal of complete celibacy. Sexual relations are doubtful in that they provide pleasure for the personality; they constitute a fall, a sin, because they are a service of the personality, which, according to Tolstoy's theory, cannot be a service of God.[10] Similarly, Tolstoyan non-resistance involves not only an assertion of the spirit but a denial of the body.

2 Contradictions

The most cogent argument for non-violence is that one should love all men equally, and that it is hypocrisy to claim that one loves a man whom one is trying to kill. This claim, which is sometimes made, can have its origin only in a dualistic view of human nature like that taken by Tolstoy. "I love your soul, but this does not prevent me from destroying your body, if I think it necessary to do so." Tolstoy himself regarded this attitude as hypocritical, for by his reasoning only a mistaken belief in the good of the personality would ever lead one to think it necessary to take life. No real good, according to him, can possibly be gained by violence. But in that case nothing at all is worth doing except preaching.

One can only withdraw from such a position by saying that

---

[10] "Afterword" to *The Kreutzer Sonata*.

in murder some real value is denied the victim. What should keep one from murder, therefore, is not the belief that the good of the personality is illusory, but the opposite of that belief; and this applies to every act of murder however it is motivated, including killing to prevent killing. Even if one thinks that a man is bent on murder, by murdering him one denies the value one is seeking to defend.

Does this mean that non-resistance should, after all, be accepted as a principle? If one sees some value in the personality, one is placed like Camus' rebel, who cannot absolutely claim not to kill without accepting, once and for all, evil and murder, but who cannot agree to kill, since the inverse reasoning which would justify murder and violence would also destroy the reasons for his insurrection.[11] And to defend non-resistance, as Tolstoy does at times,[12] on the grounds that it is the only means of putting an end to evil and murder, is to defend it by virtue of its consequences, as one foresees them, and not as an absolute principle.

The difficulties into which his dualism led Tolstoy have been carefully examined by Plekhanov, who quotes chiefly from the *Confession*, and from a collection of thoughts and aphorisms taken from Tolstoy's private correspondence, called *Ripe Ears*. Plekhanov points out how, in Tolstoy's despair, concern neither for his own well-being nor for that of the people could fill the void in his soul, so that he was compelled to turn his eyes to heaven, to find in God's will the answer to the question, "Why do I live?" [13] Plekhanov emphasises Tolstoy's consequent contrasting of the worldly and temporal with the eternal, and his disregard of the body in the name of the spirit; indeed, it is on this contrasting of the eternal with the temporal that the teaching of non-resistance to evil is based. And Plekhanov's comment is that, if the inner world of man is absolutely independent of external conditions, then there is no necessity whatever to affect these conditions in the interests of the inner world.

[11] *L'Homme Révolté*, v, translated as *The Rebel* by Anthony Bower. London (Hamish Hamilton), 1953.
[12] *The Kingdom of God is Within You*, x.
[13] "From Here to Here", II, *L. N. Tolstoy v russkoy kritike*, ed. Bychkov.

But having convicted Tolstoy of quietism and, on the evidence of *Ripe Ears*, of a reluctance even to proselytise, he suddenly says:

> But in that case what is the meaning of the famous Tolstoyan *I Cannot Be Silent*? What is the meaning of that sermon of his against the death penalty, which attracted to him the fervent sympathies of people in all countries of the civilized world? Only that Tolstoy was not always a Tolstoyan. Only that, having proclaimed the independence of the external world of man from the inner, he was obliged at times to acknowledge its dependence. Only that, having declared the control of existence by consciousness to be unnecessary and impossible, he was obliged to acknowledge both its possibility and its necessity. In other words, only that his opposition of "the eternal" and "the temporal" did not withstand the criticism of life, and that at times he could not himself help repudiating this opposition. To put it another way, Tolstoy appeared to his contemporaries to be a great teacher of life only when he repudiated his own teaching about life.[14]

Precisely. Indeed, Tolstoy's horror of killing is so deep that it is merely by deduction from his theory that one can say that to him the state of the murderer's soul is the only terrible thing about murder. He is revolted by the outrage that is done to the victim, as the article *I Cannot Be Silent* bears witness; and this revulsion testifies to an awareness of a value in the animal personality that is not accounted for in the theorising of *On Life*. It is to this awareness that his best passages are due. *What Then Must We Do?* and *Resurrection* reveal an enormous pity for the oppressed, and this pity, which is inherent in his protest against oppression, is responsible for the confusion of ideas of which Plekhanov speaks. Tolstoy, he says, was too much alive to be at peace in the dead land of quietism; but the more he strove to tear himself away from it, the more confused he became in the most desperate and tormenting contradictions; as soon as he overstepped the boundaries of that barren land of quietism, the insurmountable logic of his doctrine, based on the contrasting of the eternal

---

[14] "A Confusion of Ideas", i and ii.

with the temporal and the spirit with the body, forced him to return to it.

Pity in Tolstoy immediately provokes a sense of shame. This can be illustrated by several instances in *What Then Must We Do?*, of which the following is one. This passage needs to be quoted in full, because it is by recreating a total impression that Tolstoy conveys his sense of pity. The passage, moreover, anticipates the mood of much of *Resurrection*.

Last year, in March, I was returning home late one evening. Turning from Zubov street to Khamovniki side-street I saw some black spots on the snow of the Virgin's Field. Something was moving there. I should not have paid attention to it if a policeman standing at the entrance to the side-street had not shouted in the direction of the black spots:
'Vasili! Why don't you bring her?'
'She won't come!' replied a voice from there, and after that the black spots moved towards the policeman.
I stopped and asked him what it was. He said:
'They have arrested the wenches at the Rzhanov House and taken them to the police-station. This one lagged behind, you see she won't move.'
A yard-porter in a sheepskin coat was fetching her. She walked in front and he kept pushing her from behind. We, the porter, the policeman, and I, were all wearing winter things, but she had only her dress on. In the dusk I could only make out a brown dress, and a kerchief on her head and neck. She was short, as starvelings are, with short legs and a disproportionately broad ill-shaped figure.
'Now, carrion, we're waiting for you. Get along, I say! I'll give it you!' shouted the policeman. It was plain he was tired and had lost patience with her. She went a few steps and again stopped. The elderly yard-porter, a good-natured fellow (I know him personally), pulled her by the arm:
'There, I'll teach you to stop! Go on!' he said, pretending to be angry. She staggered and began to speak in a grating voice. Every sound she uttered was a false note, hoarse and squeaking.
'Now then! What are you shoving for? I'll get there!'
'You'll freeze,' said the porter.
'Our kind don't freeze. I'm a hot 'un.'
She meant it as a jest but it sounded like abuse. Near the

lamp-post that stands not far from the gate of our house she again stopped and leant—almost fell—against the wooden fence of the yard, and began fumbling in her skirts with clumsy be-numbed fingers. They again shouted at her, but she only muttered and went on with what she was doing. In one hand she held a cigarette bent like an arc, and in the other some sulphur matches. I stopped, ashamed to go past her though also ashamed to stand and look on. At last I made up my mind and went up to her. She leant with her shoulder against the wooden fence, and vainly trying to strike the sulphur matches against it threw them away. I looked at her face. She was a starveling, but it seemed to me no longer young. I supposed her to be about thirty. She had a dirty-coloured face, small, dim, and drunken eyes, a knob-shaped nose, crooked slobbering lips that turned down at the corners, and a short strand of dry hair showed from under her kerchief. Her figure was long and flat and her hands and feet stumpy. I stopped opposite her. She looked at me and smirked, as if to say she knew what I was thinking about.

I felt I had to say something to her, and I wished to show her that I pitied her.

'Are your parents alive?' I asked.

She laughed hoarsely, then suddenly stopped and, raising her brows, looked at me.

'Are your parents alive?' I repeated.

She smirked with an expression which seemed to say: 'You have found a queer thing to ask about!'

'I have a mother,' she said. 'What is it to you?'

'And how old are you?'

'Over fifteen,' said she, promptly answering a question she was evidently accustomed to.

'Now, get on! We shall freeze to death with you here, blast you!' shouted the policeman, and she staggered away from the fence and swaying to and fro went down Khamovniki street to the police-station, while I turned in at the gate, entered the house, and asked if my daughters had come home. I was told that they had been to a party, had enjoyed themselves very much, had returned, and were already asleep.[15]

Pity for the girl and horror at her condition—at the slow destruction of a personality—give rise to shame, because Tolstoy was a member of the parasitic upper class, whose existence was

---

[15] *What Then Must We Do ?*, xxiv.

the cause of the degradation of others. The conclusion of *What Then Must We Do?* is that all possession of property should be renounced and that every man should labour like a peasant, it being incumbent on every man to share in the struggle with nature for the support of life. But circumstances —in particular his wife's refusal to allow Tolstoy's estates to be surrendered to the peasants—prevented him from fulfilling his own teaching, so that, although he knew he was doing the right thing in remaining at Yasnaya Polyana with his wife, to whom, as a compromise, he had handed over his property, there was little abatement in his self-contempt. And self-contempt in Tolstoy is involved in the contrasting of the temporal with the eternal. As has been seen, through some perversity of logic, despising himself and his material status, he formed a doctrine of indifference to material conditions and to the well-being of the personality, thereby in theory abolishing the grounds of that pity for the oppressed which is inherent in his protest. As *What Then Must We Do?* is a revolutionary treatise advocating a specific programme, this doctrine is not evident in it.

An example Plekhanov takes of Tolstoy's temporarily leaving the barren land of quietism is his famine-relief work in 1892, when he was very active collecting money, buying grain and feeding thousands of people. But Plekhanov then quotes from a letter in which Tolstoy expresses a sense of shame and the conviction, confirmed by his activities, that with money one can do nothing but evil.[16] Apparently Plekhanov takes this conviction as exemplifying Tolstoy's quietistic tendency and his doctrinal indifference to material affairs. Tolstoy would not have been ashamed of himself, he says, if he had been able to be consistent; and to be consistent, he should have expounded the five commandments to the starving peasants, instead of feeding them. But in this case Tolstoy was ashamed, not so much because he was giving material aid rather than preaching, as because he was merely "making a pipe of himself": "distributing the vomit thrown up by the rich", giving money while remaining a social parasite, and therefore not assisting in the only way one can honestly materially assist a

[16] "A Confusion of Ideas", IV.

man: by personal labour, as he himself had helped the widow Anisya.[17] The frustration of his desire to separate himself from the gentry, and support himself by his own labour in solidarity with the peasants, was very tragic. There is terrible anguish, in *I Cannot Be Silent*, in the acknowledgment that he belongs to that class which defends itself by means of the gallows against the people it oppresses.

Plekhanov reconsiders *I Cannot Be Silent* in another article, having previously referred to it only in relation to the question of proselytism; and the Marxist ultimately condemns it for its quietism. Tolstoy chose, if it were impossible to be anything but a victim or an executioner, to be a victim. In suggesting that the well-soaped noose should be put on him too and that he too should be pushed off a bench and hanged, Tolstoy was only repeating, in Plekhanov's opinion, that idea of his that, when a mother is flogging her child, then we—not having the moral right to snatch the child from her—may only stand in his place. The executioners continued their work, as if they had not heard Tolstoy's request, "Hang me too".

In the class struggle, all Tolstoy could do was to call upon the exploited to refrain from violence, and the exploiters to repent. The only permissible means, according to him, of campaigning for the abolition of the death penalty consisted, as Plekhanov points out, in "impressing on all people, especially the hangmen's managers and those who approve of them", a right understanding of man and of his relation to the world that surrounds him; so that it turns out that we no longer even need to stand in the way of the mother who flogs her child: "it is enough to acquaint her with the religious teaching of Count Tolstoy".[18]

Plekhanov spoils his case by overstating it. He says:

> Instead of analysing the mutual relations of people, Tolstoy, who was, in essence, absolutely indifferent to those relations and interested exclusively in himself, analysed his own psychic life.[19]

[17] Aylmer Maude, *The Life of Tolstoy*, Vol. II, Ch. XII, pp. 298 and 304, and Ch. VIII, p. 213.
[18] "Karl Marx and Leo Tolstoy", 1911, II, *L. N. Tolstoy v russkoy kritike*, ed. Bychkov.
[19] Quoted by Bychkov in his introduction to *L. N. Tolstoy v russkoy kritike*, p. 43.

This is patently untrue, and can be refuted by reference to *What Then Must We Do?*

What Then Must We Do? was completed three years before *The Kreutzer Sonata* and a year before *On Life.* In it Tolstoy does not develop his thesis by arguing from a specific philosophy of life, as he does in the 1890's in *The Kingdom of God is Within You* and *The First Step*; Christianity is merely vindicated in passing and implied in the conclusion. Non-violence is claimed, at the end of the discussion of money, to be the only remedy of injustice;[20] it is not asserted at the beginning as a principle, as it is in *What I Believe* as well as in *The Kingdom of God is Within You.* In *What Then Must We Do?* Tolstoy begins by describing an iniquity and looks for a solution; he does not start with a solution ready-made. Compared with it, the argument in *The First Step*, which moves from general instruction about the righteous life to a description of a particular wrong—cruelty to animals—is back-to-front, since it suggests that one should abstain from meat primarily to promote one's own blessedness, vegetarianism being the first step in the infinite road to perfection. *What Then Must We Do?* begins with a sense of shame and outrage at injustice, and goes on to assert the claims of the oppressed; and the welfare of the personality, far from being denied, is the very thing Tolstoy is trying to secure in seeking for just principles. He says, for instance, that, just as the slave has an innate right to seek his own welfare rather than that of his owner, so each man has an innate right to live on the land and with his personal or communal tools to produce things he considers useful for himself.[21]

In *What I Believe* marriage is held to be holy and obligatory;[22] in the last chapter of *What Then Must We Do?* the bearing of children is regarded as the fulfilment of God's will, and the joys of love are hymned. Aylmer Maude accounts for the expression of the opposite opinion in *The Kreutzer Sonata* and its *Afterword* by referring to Tolstoy's quarrels with his wife over the disposal of his property, which caused him to feel that sexual love and marriage form an obstacle to right life and as

---

[20] *What Then Must We Do?*, XXI and XXII.
[21] *Ibid.*, XVII.
[22] *What I Believe*, XII.

I

such should be shunned by a Christian.[23] This is a kind explanation, but it is not a complete one; for, whatever light our
knowledge of Tolstoy's private life may throw on the attitude
that underlies *The Kreutzer Sonata*, it is clear that the ideas
expressed therein follow inevitably from his belief in the need
for the renunciation of personal well-being. When writing
What I Believe, he was not aware that the ideal of celibacy is
the logical deduction to make from that belief—a belief that
is not enunciated in *What Then Must We Do ?*, in the last chapter
of which the argument moves on a tide of impulses that involve
joy in physical life and are not yet changed into the loathing
that in *The Kreutzer Sonata* is bolstered by teleology.

[23] Footnote to his translation of *What I Believe*, vi.

V

The Kingdom of God: Tolstoy and the Grand Inquisitor

THE obvious criticism to make of Plekhanov's approach to Tolstoy is that it is one-sided, making merely a passing tribute to his genius as an artist. But, whereas Plekhanov drew a sharp distinction between Tolstoy's art and moral philosophy, Dr George Steiner's discussion of the latter is based on the belief that it is rooted in the quality and techniques of his art. This belief causes Dr Steiner to overlook too much—"I will restrict myself to those aspects of Tolstoy's metaphysics which can be most securely related to the poetics of the Tolstoyan novel," he says[1]—and, when taken to extremes, it produces conclusions that are demonstrably false.

His *Tolstoy or Dostoevsky* effectively contrasts the dramatic genius of Dostoevsky with the epic quality of the Tolstoyan novel, and it is an illuminating study of the relations between the artists' styles and their philosophies. What Berdyaev called the "insoluble controversy" between the two novelists, the antagonism between "fundamental conceptions of existence",[2] is examined. But at the end of the book, albeit tentatively and provisionally, Dr Steiner attempts to read the Legend of the Grand Inquisitor as an allegory of the confrontation between Dostoevsky and Tolstoy,[3] and suggests that the prophet of Yasnaya Polyana resembled Dostoevsky's priest. This surprising conclusion is possible only because, in the pages that lead up to the comparison, Dr Steiner has misrepresented Tolstoy's ideas, revealing a fundamental misunderstanding of his religious teaching, and it is just this false image of Tolstoy thus created that is like the fanatical Inquisitor.

Dr Steiner emphasises the rational side of Tolstoy, and

[1] *Tolstoy or Dostoevsky: An Essay in Contrast*, Ch. 4, iii, p. 249.
[2] *Ibid.*, Ch. 4, vii, p. 333.　　　　　　　　[3] *Ibid.*, p. 328.

points to his rejection of belief in heaven as another world where
justice will be meted out, and where those who have suffered
destitution and oppression patiently in this world will be re-
warded with bliss.[4] Of course, such a belief is irrational and
can serve, moreover, as a justification of an oppressive social
system—as Tolstoy saw, when, in his last years, he devoted his
rhetoric to trying to destroy the Tsarist regime by persuading
people not to own land, work for the government, or exploit
the peasants, in order that there might be established

> an order of life in which the discord, deception, and violence
> that now rule will be replaced by free accord, by truth, and by
> the brotherly love of one for another.

And of course, as Dr Steiner says, Tolstoy's great novels cele-
brate the reality of life on earth in time and space. "The art
of Tolstoy is anti-Platonic," he writes—apparently without
realising that what he says of Tolstoy's art is in effect the opposite of Axelrod's criticism of his thought: that he proclaimed
life as death and death as life.[5] Dr Steiner's argument consists
in saying that, because Tolstoy was rationalistic and believed
that common sense and "the inner light" would indicate to
him the true meaning of the Gospels, and because he rejected
the dogmas of the churches, was an artist of nature rather than
of the spirit, and demanded that a just and peaceful arrange-
ment of society should be attained in this life on earth, he is
therefore to be associated with the Comtians and all the
enemies of the open and imperfect society. On the one side
Dr Steiner puts the liberals, who distrust final solutions and
believe that some measure of injustice and absurdity in human
affairs is unavoidable; and on the other side he puts Anabap-
tists, Adamites, Saint-Simonians, Comtians, Soviet Communists,
Tolstoy, and the "thousand-year" *Reich* of National Socialism.
The idea of the Kingdom of God, he says, is central to this
distinction, because either that Kingdom exists in another
world where there is redemptive judgment—in which case we
may accept the persistence of evil in this world—or there is no

---

[4] *Tolstoy or Dostoevsky*, Ch. 4, iii, pp. 253-9.
[5] "Tolstoy's Inner Tragedy as the Basis of his Doctrine", xv, *O Tolstom*, ed.
V. M. Friche.

other world and we must establish the Kingdom of God, understood as justice and equality, in this.

To accomplish this, we may have to overthrow existing society. Cruelty, intolerance, fanatical rigour become temporary virtues in the service of the revolutionary ideal. History may have to pass through Armageddon or decades of political terror. But in the end the state shall wither away and man shall awake once again in the first garden.

Such a generalisation passes over the possibility of there being a significant difference between those who have scruples, and those who do not have scruples, about what methods to use, among those who have wanted to establish the Kingdom of God on earth. Yet it might be objected that Dr Steiner, in speaking in general terms, is only reflecting on the idea that "Tolstoy envisaged a terrestrial Kingdom of God", as he puts it, whereas Dostoevsky asserted not only that such a thing is impossible, but also that the attempt to establish it would result in atheism and political bestiality. However, it should be pointed out that, though Dr Steiner attempts to outline Tolstoy's conception of the Kingdom of God, he never refers to *The Kingdom of God is Within You*, a major work, in which, as elsewhere, the ideal of non-resistance to evil by violence is strenuously insisted upon; and if he had examined this ideal and its basis, he would have found not only that Tolstoy indisputably did scruple about methods, and that the "commissar's" doctrine that the end justifies the means was anathema to him, as he was, in Mr Koestler's terms, a "yogi", but also that, although with part of his being he may have longed for a terrestrial Kingdom of God, he could not, strictly speaking, accept such an idea.

Dr Steiner writes that Tolstoy envisaged a terrestrial Kingdom of God: as it says in St John's Gospel,

> the work of God "consists in believing in the life He has given you". With a sombre instinct Tolstoy felt that He would give no other.

But what did Tolstoy understand by life? His distinction between false and true life, between personal life and life in the son of man, is, as we have seen, the expression of a metaphysical system, according to which life is fulfilled only in death. Dr Steiner says:

> Tolstoy's conception of the Kingdom of God arose directly out of his stubborn attempts to entrap the death-drawn soul and to retain it everlastingly within the confines of the tangible world.

But Tolstoy wrote that Christ's teaching demands the fusion of the divine essence or nature that exists in each man's soul with the will of God, and that this fusion involves freeing the divine nature from the animal nature.[6] And such was his own teaching too. If one makes logical deductions from Tolstoy's metaphysics, one finds that, in spite of his protests against oppression, and longing for a new, peaceful, and harmonious way of life, a terrestrial Kingdom of God is not consistent with those metaphysics.

This may seem strange to one who is familiar with the revolutionary ideas of *What Then Must We Do?* (though this work too repudiates the use of force), and with Tolstoy's later advocacy of the Henry George single-tax system.[7] Tolstoy wrote much in favour of Henry George and his system of reform, although the administration of such a system would require at least tax-collectors and civil servants. And in a little-known article called *Patriotism and Government*—the theme of which is that people should destroy those instruments of violence called governments, by acknowledging all patriotism to be harmful, disgraceful, and immoral—in reply to the objection that, if governments are abolished, there will be no laws, property, courts of justice, police, or popular education, Tolstoy suddenly says:

> The abolition of the organization of government formed to do violence does not at all involve the abolition of what is reasonable and good, and therefore not based on violence, in laws or law courts, or in property, or in police regulations, or in financial arrangements, or in popular education. On the contrary, the absence of the brutal power of government which is needed

---

[6] *The Kingdom of God is Within You*, IV.

[7] Letters on Henry George, to T. M. Bondarev and a German propagandist, 1897, published by Aylmer Maude in Tolstoy's *Recollections and Essays*; *A Great Iniquity*; *Resurrection*, Part II, Chs. VI and IX.

only for its own support, will facilitate a more just and reasonable social organization, needing no violence. Courts of justice, and public affairs, and popular education, will all exist to the extent to which they are really needed by the people, but in a form which will not involve the evils contained in the present form of government. Only that will be destroyed which was evil and hindered the free expression of the people's will.

This is an odd concession. The fourth commandment is, "Do not go to law", and, when put in the form, "Do not resist evil by violence" ("*nasiliem*"), is regarded as the key to Christ's teaching. "*Nasilie*" also means "coercion" or "compulsion"; and law courts and police regulations are inconceivable without a basis of coercion. While one welcomes this paragraph for its moderation, in contrast with Tolstoy's tendency to push the principle of non-resistance to ridiculous extremes, one cannot but recognise that it was written in a moment of weakness, as its internal contradiction suggests. Beside it can be put the following remarks, made by Tolstoy in conversation, as a reflection on the essential nature of his ethical system:

> For a true Christian neither Henry George exists nor anything. All his efforts are directed only towards what is in his power, that is towards himself, and at the same time there lives in him an unshakable conviction that there is no more worth-while activity for the world than this work on himself. Henry George is a concession, a weakness. Not to kill people is good; not to kill people or animals or parasites is better. To live honourably with one's wife in marriage is good; to live chastely with her in marriage is still better; to live without a wife in complete chastity is still better. Similarly: some say that for the good of the people a gallows has to be put in every town; others say, "No, socialist planning is better"; and we say that Henry George is still better. But, I repeat, this is weakness . . .[8]

Dr Steiner makes no reference to the theory expressed in *The Kreutzer Sonata*, xi, that, when the aim of life is achieved—that is, when the Kingdom of God is attained—life should come to an end. Mankind will achieve unity but then cease to exist. This means that his reference to "a world which the Shigalovs

---

[8] Conversation with Nazhivin, quoted by Axelrod in "Tolstoy's Inner Tragedy", vii.

or the Tolstoys have made materially perfect and in which men look earthward with the eyes of contented brutes",[9] is unwarranted and unfair.

Again, Dr Steiner speaks of

> the belief of Tolstoy and of all social radicals that men may be persuaded to love one another through reason and utilitarian enlightenment.[10]

Not only did Tolstoy teach that love is the result of spiritual regeneration from within, and not of persuasion, but also, in *The Kingdom of God is Within You*, IV, he expressly dissociated himself from the Positivists, Communists, and Socialists. He argued that the love for humanity which they want cannot be genuine, for they do not understand that love that does not originate in the divine nature—which they deny—can only be animal love and cannot, therefore, be extended to the whole of humanity. Far from being antagonistic to Dostoevsky in this respect, Tolstoy, who wrote, "Humanity is a fiction and it is impossible to love it", would have agreed with him when he said, as Dr Steiner quotes,

> that love of mankind is unthinkable, unintelligible and *altogether impossible without the accompanying faith in the immortality of man's soul.* . . . I even assert and venture to say that love of mankind *in general, as an idea,* is one of the most incomprehensible ideas for the human mind.

Admittedly, Tolstoy in a sense denied that immortality in *What I Believe*, VIII, but in *On Life* he asserted it, saying quite clearly that true life is not what takes place in time and space.

Axelrod appreciated the opposition between Tolstoy and social radicals on this point, for she quoted the words, "Humanity is a fiction and it is impossible to love it", and said:

> I emphasise the fact that Tolstoy *consciously and in principle* regarded altruism and humanism *as a fiction,* and attacked socialist ethics precisely because they take these social principles as their point of departure.[11]

Then, holding that the defining conceptions in Tolstoy's religion, God, the Good, and brotherly love among men, are

[9] *Tolstoy or Dostoevsky*, Ch. 4, v, pp. 296-7.
[10] *Ibid.*, p. 295.   [11] "Tolstoy's Inner Tragedy", XII.

interchangeable, Dr Steiner says that, through a gradual process of equation, we arrive at an anthropology of mortal greatness in which men have created God in their own image.[12] It is true that in Tolstoy God often appears to be equated with man's rational nature, but that nature is always distinguished from man's animal nature; and it is in the light of this distinction that Tolstoy's conception of brotherly love must be understood.

Dr Steiner associates Tolstoy and the Grand Inquisitor because, as he sees them, they were both rationalistic, paternalistic ascetics, bent on establishing the Kingdom of God on earth.[13] He regards Dostoevsky's Inquisitor as of the same type as Shigalov in *The Possessed*, and his vision of the total state as a prophecy of the totalitarian regimes of the twentieth century. Quite rightly he understands *1984* as an epilogue to Dostoevsky's Legend—and we recall Orwell's hostility to Tolstoy's moralising: the perception that it takes all sorts to make a world is essential to freedom, and Tolstoy lost this perception when he entered his religious period—hence his "spiritual bullying".[14]

However, the following differences between Tolstoy and the Inquisitor need to be pointed out.

The Inquisitor claimed that he loved humanity better than Christ did, because he regarded men as weak, ignoble, vicious creatures who would never be able to cope with the freedom Christ gave them. Tolstoy wrote:

> A Christian is free from every human authority by the fact that he regards the divine law of love implanted in the soul of every man, and of which Christ has made us conscious, as the sole guide of his life and of the lives of others.[15]

Tolstoyan anarchism is based on the assumption that everyone has the strength to live by that law.

The Inquisitor strove to release men from suffering by providing *miracle*, *mystery*, and *authority*—that is, by answering the

[12] *Tolstoy or Dostoevsky*, Ch 4, iii, p. 266.
[13] *Ibid.*, Ch 4, vii, pp. 333-43.
[14] "Lear, Tolstoy, and the Fool", 1947, reprinted in *Inside the Whale and Other Essays*. Harmondsworth (Penguin) 1962.
[15] *The Kingdom of God is Within You*, ix.

psychological needs of weak creatures. Tolstoy strove to destroy the cause of suffering, which he believed to be error, by "the activity of true life",[16] which involves a true appreciation of man's essential duality, and the submission of the animal personality to reasonable consciousness.

Miracle. Tolstoy's *What Men Live By* makes contrary assertions to those of the Inquisitor concerning bread and worship. Men live by love, and it is not given to each to know his own needs. God wants men to live united, but in love, in the spirit, to which each submits his personality and his appetite, not in worship of the hand that provides the bread to satisfy that appetite.

Mystery. Tolstoy rejected the miracles and mysteries of the New Testament, not only because he found the miracles unconvincing, but also because he thought that inculcation of the dogmas of the churches perverts the mind and destroys freedom of conscience.[17]

Authority. While it is true that Tolstoy wished all men to be united, and the image of ants appealed to him—his brother's Ant Brotherhood [18]—yet, as Dr Steiner admits, his "hopes were founded on non-violence". A world state, ruled by those who have taken possession of men's consciences and in whose hands their bread is, would have been loathsome to him; for, according to his teaching, no one should have that domination over men's consciences or control of the food-supply. Of course, there is a socialist rather than an anarchist tendency in the advocacy of the Henry George single-tax system; but not only did Tolstoy, as Dr Steiner notes, glimpse "that possibility of disaster which haunted Herzen and Dostoevsky", prophesying that, if there was a revolution in Russia, a new despotism would displace the old; but also the massive rhetoric of *The Kingdom of God is Within You*, especially Chapter x, makes it clear that no sort of rule, domination or government, involving the slightest use of force, would have been acceptable to him. "It even seems ridiculous to speak of Christians ruling", and, "*The evil always domineer over the good and inflict violence on them*". To rule is to use force ("*nasilovat'* "); to use force on a man is

---

[16] *On Life*, xxxv.   [17] *What is Religion?*, xiii.
[18] Aylmer Maude, *The Life of Tolstoy*, Vol. i, Ch. ii, pp. 18-19.

to do to him what he does not want done, and what you would not want done to yourself; and therefore to rule is to do wrong. So we are left with consideration of the moral compulsion and spiritual bullying that there is in Tolstoy. Indeed, Dr Steiner refers to what we know of Tolstoy's temperament— his "aristocracy" and "paternalism". In spite of his rejection of temporal authority, Tolstoy himself "loved men from above". Almost the only valid points in the whole of Dr Steiner's comparison are this, and the points that Tolstoy in effect complained, like the Inquisitor, that the New Testament is "exceptional, vague and enigmatic", and that, like him, he was a lonely, rationalistic ascetic, who lived to an old age.

What is wrong is Dr Steiner's conclusion:

> But one can say this: both the Grand Inquisitor and the later Tolstoy stood in mysterious rivalry to their images of God. Both were intent upon establishing utopian kingdoms in which God would be a rare or unwelcome guest. In their different ways, they exemplified one of Dostoevsky's essential theses: that humanitarian socialism is, fatally, a prelude to atheism.

This is wrong because, however vague Tolstoy's conception of God was, his ideal, as has been shown, was not to create an earthly happiness to which God would be irrelevant or unwelcome, but to be absorbed into God by means of a gradual process which Axelrod described as destruction of the will to live.

Not to speak of the prejudice that is evident in the last chapter of Dr Steiner's book,[19] one can take his comparison of

---

[19] The chapter suggests that Dr Steiner condemns Tolstoy's moral philosophy not so much because he sees it as a threat to liberal values, as because he really prefers Dostoevsky's irrationalism. Take the following for example: "But in the playhouse of the Grand Inquisitor there could be no tragic drama. 'As soon as man has vanquished nature,' announced Lunacharsky, the first Soviet commissar of education, 'religion becomes superfluous; thereupon the sense of the tragic shall vanish from our lives.' Everyone, with the exception of a handful of incurable madmen, would know and rejoice in the certainty that twice two equals four, that Claude Bernard had penetrated to the centre of the vascular system, and that Count Tolstoy was building model schools on his estates. Foremost among the insane would be Dostoevsky and his principal characters. They stand in radical antagonism to worldly utopias, to all paradigms of secular reform which would lull man's soul into a sleep of comfort and material satiety, thus banishing from it the tragic sense of life." (Ch. 4, v, pp. 299-300.) One has to point out that Tolstoy objected to compulsory education and to

Tolstoy and the Grand Inquisitor as a warning of how far it is possible to go astray in the criticism of Tolstoy if his dualism is disregarded. One would have thought, indeed, that it could not be disregarded, as it is fundamental to his religious teaching and manifest in his art.

Plekhanov wrote:

> All his preaching rested upon the contrasting of "the spirit" with "the body", and "the eternal" with "the temporal". This opposition leads inevitably to the conclusion that man's happiness "does not depend on external causes", which always have, of course, only a "temporal" character, and Tolstoy not only is not afraid of this conclusion, but repeats it with unshaken conviction, especially where it marks the contrast between his teaching and that of the socialists. Socialists believe that the happiness of man in society depends on an "external cause" called the social system.[20]

This is almost enough to refute Dr Steiner's final point, which is that, with the triumph of Shigalovism in Russia, Dostoevsky was rejected by the new inquisitors, whereas Tolstoy "was securely enshrined in the revolutionary pantheon".[21] One cannot help suspecting that Dr Steiner knows very little about Soviet criticism of Tolstoy;[22] he mentions the fact that Lenin called Tolstoy "a mirror of the Russian revolution", without

---

compulsory attendance at lessons by pupils, maintaining that the more freedom that is possible in a school, the better that school is; that he thought that the pupils or their parents should choose what is to be taught, and that children learn best when they are merry and their curiosity is excited; and that he regarded as illegitimate and sterile the deliberate attempt made at day schools, boarding schools, and universities alike, by members of the upper and middle classes of society, to mould the characters of the young as they wish. Accordingly, his educational practice, far from being despotic, illiberal, or intolerant, had much in common with that of Mr A. S. Neill and Bertrand Russell.

Most of Tolstoy's articles on education appeared in his magazine *Yasnaya Polyana* in 1862. See Aylmer Maude, *The Life of Tolstoy*, Vol. 1, Chs. vii and viii, pp. 240-78, and Ch. x, pp. 332-48; see also Sir Isaiah Berlin, "Tolstoy and Enlightenment", *Encounter*, Vol. xvi, (Feb. 1961).

[20] "More about Tolstoy" ("*Yeshchë o Tolstom*"), 1911, 1, reprinted in *L. N. Tolstoy v russkoy kritike, Sbornik statey*, ed. S. P. Bychkov.

[21] *Tolstoy or Dostoevsky*, Ch. 4, viii, p. 345.

[22] The subject has been studied by Professor Gleb Struve in *The Russian Review*, Vol. 19, (April 1960), "Tolstoy in Soviet Criticism". My quotations from Lenin are in Professor Struve's translation.

adding that in the same article Lenin also called Tolstoy "an effete, hysterical weakling . . . who beats his breast in public" and preaches religion and non-resistance. Even if Tolstoy was enshrined in the revolutionary pantheon, it is not clear what inference can be drawn, since he wrote enough to show that he would have loathed both the aims and the methods of the Soviet government, as Lenin well knew. Lenin said, for example:

> In our days any attempt to idealize Tolstoy's teaching, to justify or tone down his doctrine of 'non-resistance', his appeals to the 'Spirit', his call for 'moral self-improvement', his teaching about 'conscience' and about 'universal love', his preaching of asceticism and quietism, etc., would result in most direct and far-reaching harm.[23]

Tolstoy's principles are indisputably incompatible with Bolshevik theory and practice. Any argument designed, like Dr Steiner's, to associate him with Shigalovism would have to ignore his dualism and consider, in the examination of his tracts, only those passages where, as Plekhanov would say, Tolstoy is not a Tolstoyan.

[23] "L. N. Tolstoy and his Epoch", 1911, *L. N. Tolstoy v russkoy kritike*, ed. Bychkov.

VI

Resurrection

1 Introduction

"RESURRECTION" is a protest against oppression and a revolt on the part of the spirit against aspects of nature. Tolstoyism, a religion of submission to the will of God, the origin of all, is a peculiar blend of protest and consent.[1] The metaphysical consent to disease, suffering, and death, which is inherent in Tolstoy's dualism,[2] is, however, scarcely apparent in *Resurrection*, which treats of evils of a human origin. Apart from saying that Nekhlyudov felt, in the coincidence by which he was on the jury at Katusha's trial, the hand of God as Master convicting him of sin,[3] Tolstoy does not appear to see in the particular occurrences of the story any design of a guiding destiny, the resurrection that takes place being entirely inward, and requiring one to struggle in spirit against the animal forces that cause the course of events to lead to misery and oppression; nor does he commit himself on the question of the ultimate meaning of the totality of events in the world.

The work that our life accomplishes, the whole of this work, the meaning of it, is not, nor can be, intelligible to me. What were

---

[1] There is a criticism of *Resurrection* by L. I. Axelrod. Her approach is to ask why the novel has the title it has, and why it concludes with a reading of the Gospels. In answer she gives a summary of Tolstoy's doctrine, as it is in *On Life*. Thus she sees *Resurrection* as a revolt against nature and as an expression of metaphysical consent, leading to quietism and to indifference to the suffering of others, but not at all as a protest against oppression. She maintains that the merciless social criticism which there is in the novel is intended to show that life in general is worthless, and that Nekhlyudov is shown the "hell" of this world in order that he may be guided to Nirvana. Axelrod, angry at and hurt by the portraits of the revolutionaries Novodvorov and Vera Dukhova (Bogodukhovskaya), is blind to the pity that has been noticed in the novel, and makes no mention of Henry George in her essay. The essay is reprinted in *O Tolstom: Literaturno-kritichesky sbornik*, ed. V. M. Friche.

[2] *On Life*, xxxiv.   [3] Part I, Ch. xxii.

my aunts for? Why did Nikolenka Irtenyev die?—while I am still living? What was Katusha for? And my madness? Why that war? Why my subsequent lawless life? To understand it, to understand the whole of the Master's will, is not in my power. But to do His will that is written in my conscience, is in my power—and what it is I know for certain. And when I am fulfilling it I have sureness and peace.[4]

Tolstoy concludes by saying that the only reasonable meaning of life lies in man's duty to fulfil the five commandments of the Sermon on the Mount, for in these laws is expressed the Master's will. These laws are discovered by the spirit, but, while they follow from a definite relation to life, they cannot of themselves give meaning to phenomena or events. Events generally appear to be important to Tolstoy in so far as they degrade or elevate the spirit of man: prostitution and the prison system destroy it; Nekhlyudov seeks to restore it in Katusha. The former, depraving occurrences are the result of human sinfulness, that is, of transgression of the will of the Master, Who speaks to the conscience. But the deafness to conscience, the suppression of the spiritual ego, can be due only to the urges of the animal ego, assisted by various distracting influences.[5] Hence the revolt against certain aspects of nature; everything is to be subordinate to the spirit, to which man's lower nature is a potential source of danger. Such a revolt is, in fact, inevitable as soon as one asks the meaning of life, for that question divides everything else off over against consciousness and demands that it should satisfy consciousness. Tolstoy defines life by what we know in ourselves, with the result that generally the unconscious is not valued for what it is in itself.

2 Protest against Oppression

Part of the greatness of *Resurrection* lies in the force of the protest against oppression. It has the uncompromising clarity and fearlessness of the writings of Tolstoy's last period, combined with precise observation of particulars. There is remarkable singleness of purpose. A simple examination of the conditions by which lawyers, officials, prisoners, poverty-stricken peasants, and the members of fashionable society are mutually

---

[4] Part II, Ch. VIII.   [5] Part I, Ch. XIII.

involved, produces an enormous vision of evil, a vision of a depraving social system whose inevitable consequence is cannibalism.[6]

But the protest has two forms: that which it assumes when Tolstoy speaks in his own person, omniscient in the world of his novel, and that which it assumes in Nekhlyudov's reflections as he awakens to the reality of that world; and the latter is more artistically striking, the former tending to have the rigidity of propaganda. Tolstoy's own criterion can be applied here: "the religious content of art" is the expression of a definite view of life, of an outlook which permeates a whole work though the author be unconscious of it; and the author should, therefore, communicate his *Weltanschauung* without sinking to an external inculcation of any religious truth in artistic guise.[7] Tolstoy is very conscious of his own outlook, having carefully formulated it, and it is as clear in Nekhlyudov's reflections as it is in those passages where Tolstoy addresses the reader directly. The novel is tendentious throughout; yet it is not mere teaching. The sense of reality is there in the presentation both of Nekhlyudov's inner struggle and of the world around him; and his meditations are part of that experience, no less than his interviews and disputes (such as those with Rogozhinsky, where the chief interest lies not so much in the possible truth of Nekhlyudov's opinions as in the psychology of his reaction to the situation and his offensive manner).[8] But *Resurrection* is inartistic in so far as clarification at times gives place to over-simplification, inadequate and one-sided attitudes emerge, and there is a weakening in the creative flow in Part III.

In *War and Peace* and *Anna Karenina* one feels Tolstoy himself seeking for solutions to life's problems and being only one step ahead of his protagonists; in *Resurrection*, on the other hand, Nekhlyudov is discovering what Tolstoy has thought out years before.

> . . . and Nekhlyudov clearly saw that all these people were arrested, locked-up, exiled, not really because they infringed justice or behaved unlawfully, but only because they were an

---

[6] Part III, Ch. XIX.   [7] *Shakespeare and the Drama*, VII.
[8] Part II, Chs. XXXII and XXXIII.

obstacle, hindering the officials and the rich from enjoying the property they had taken away from the people.

There can be no mistake about Nekhlyudov's perception, which is in exact accord with what Tolstoy has told us in his own person. Tolstoy gives us definitive judgments on the motives of the oppressors—of those who conduct the church service in the prison, and of Ivan Mikhaylich, Wolf, Kriegsmuth, Selenin, and Toporov[9]—and he expresses these motives in their baldest and crudest form, seeming to say to the reader, "I defy you to show that their motives are any better".

But the study, for example, of Senator Wolf, "*un homme très comme il faut*", becomes more acute when Tolstoy moves from comment to dramatic representation of him as he appears to Nekhlyudov, pacing up and down the room and smoking a cigar, talking with a patronising smile and taking care not to drop the ash. "All cases are exceptional," he says. Nekhlyudov, who feels moral nausea, is confronted by an almost unbelievable self-assurance on the part of the oppressors; and it is against this self-assurance that some of Tolstoy's cleverest satire is directed. There is caustic humour combined with keen observation running through a great part of *Resurrection*: in the account of the trial and the jury, and in Nekhlyudov's frequent interviews and visits. Tolstoy goes about his task of presenting a series of portraits of the individuals whom Nekhlyudov meets, and consuming them with his scorn. Striking details, such as the ironical smile on the face of General Chervyansky,[10] bring tangibility to Nekhlyudov's experience. He is haunted by the question whether it is he that is mad, or those who consider that they are in their right minds while they judge and punish men.

Perhaps the best of these portraits is that of General Kriegsmuth. Kriegsmuth is the governor of the Petropavlov Fortress Prison, a severe and stupid old man, who practises spiritualism. Being bound by the imperial regulations, he refuses Nekhlyudov's request that scientific books might be sent to one of the prisoners; and he proceeds to enumerate

---

[9] Part I, Ch. XL, and Part II, Chs. XV, XVI, XIX, XXIII, and XXVII.
[10] Part II, Ch. XXVIII.

K

the comforts the prisoners enjoy: three courses for dinner, one of them meat, and on Sundays a fourth:

> 'God grant every Russian may live as well as they do . . .
>
> 'They get books on religious subjects, and old journals. We have a library. But they rarely read. . . . Writing, too, is not forbidden,' he continued. 'A slate is provided, and a slate pencil, so that they can write as a pastime. They can wipe the slate and write again. But they don't write, either. Oh, they very soon get quite tranquil. . . .'
>
> Nekhlyudov listened to the hoarse old voice, looked at the stiff limbs, the lustreless eyes under the grey brows, at the old, clean-shaven, flabby jaw supported by the collar of the military uniform, at the white cross this man was so proud of, chiefly because he had gained it by exceptionally cruel and extensive slaughter—and knew that it was useless to reply to the old man or to explain to him the meaning of his own words.

Having persuaded himself, as he had to, that his prisoners are all most immoral people, and so feeling that Nekhlyudov, in his concern for them, is simply misguided, the General concludes with some advice: "Best of all, go and serve; the Tsar needs honest men,—and the country."

Of course, these portraits in *Resurrection* need to be related to the structure of the novel as a whole. Kriegsmuth has to be seen as Nekhlyudov sees him when he is at this stage of his quest; the satirical study of the General is, in the organisation of the book, necessarily associated with that whole world of cruelty, indifference, and greed which is being revealed to Nekhlyudov, and which, as it is the world he himself belongs to, makes his moral revolt against it most harrowing for himself. Kriegsmuth was a comrade of Nekhlyudov's father.

But it is not necessary that everything should be seen through Nekhlyudov's eyes. Tolstoy aims at giving a true picture of prison life and, at the same time, suggesting his own definite attitude towards it. There is powerful satire, for example, in Part i, Chapter xxxix, which gives an account of a church service in the prison where Katusha (Katerina Maslova) is. The chapter is so placed that the studied mocking of the ritual derives part of its bitterness from the preceding accounts of the miseries endured by the prisoners and of

Maslova's disillusionment; though in the latter Tolstoy lapses into a kind of crude nineteenth-century melodrama, in his description of Maslova's visit at night to the railway-station where Nekhlyudov was passing through.[11] But the scene in the women's cell is very well done; there is control and precise observation; and Tolstoy is able to reveal his attitude towards what he is recounting without using his protagonist as his mouthpiece and without making any comment himself. His outlook permeates his narrative. Maslova's tears, the conversation of the prisoners, and the production of vodka lead up, in fine dramatic writing, to the fight between Korableva and the red-haired woman.[12] Revolt is implied in the horrifying realism, and comment is unnecessary. Any *explicit* protest in the novel must be related to Nekhlyudov's moral nausea, where it becomes part of his experience; otherwise Tolstoy's artistic criterion is infringed.

The basis of the protest, implied or explicit, is pity, horror, and shame. Romain Rolland called *Resurrection* "one of the most beautiful poems of compassion".[13] A very pathetic figure in the novel is Menshov, a peasant lad, imprisoned for the crime of arson of which he is innocent. While listening to his story, Nekhlyudov looked

> at the low bedstead with its straw mattress, the window with thick iron gratings, the dirty, damp wall, and at the piteous face and form of this unfortunate disfigured peasant in his prison cloak and shoes; and he felt sadder and sadder, and would have liked not to believe what this good-natured fellow was saying. It seemed too dreadful to think that people could do such a thing as to take a man, without any reason except that he himself had been injured, dress him in convict clothes, and keep him in such a horrible place.[14]

"Compassion" ("*sostradanie*"), "horror", "perplexity", and "shame" are the words used to describe Nekhlyudov's feelings. As the account of Menshov's misfortunes illustrates, the compassion takes the form of pity for, rather than sympathy with,

[11] Part I, Ch. xxxvII.   [12] Part I, Chs. xxx-xxxII.
[13] *Vie de Tolstoi*, p. 155; quoted by Professor Marc Slonim in "Four Western Writers on Tolstoy", *The Russian Review*, Vol. 19, (April 1960).
[14] Part I, Ch. LII.

the victim; Nekhlyudov cannot share Menshov's feelings, but is sorry for him, and therefore is ashamed of himself.

Resurrection is great as a study of depravity and moral revolt. When Tolstoy departs from this, the narrative is apt to lose its individuality. He is noticeably out of his depth when dealing with the political prisoners in Part III, where there is a lack of significant details, so that these characters are reported on rather than created.[15] (Exceptional, however, is Kriltsov's story of how he saw two prisoners being taken away to execution; the account is simple, but intense in its reproduction of the details that struck Kriltsov. This event is the root of his anger: "From that time I became a revolutionist." [16]) Even Simonson, who is important to the story, is wooden. Tolstoy naïvely tells us that Simonson follows his own reason,[17] without there being any suggestion of how impulses and desires may select the first principles on which reason must rely and found its arguments. Such a crude statement is the kind of thing Tolstoy was liable to be guilty of in his last period. That the answer to the problem of the whole system of misery and oppression which is revealed in the book is forgiveness, is implied by the way the problem is stated; but, having given us this solution, Tolstoy cannot resist the temptation to go on and deliver his manifesto. In the last chapter Nekhlyudov, in noting the five commandments of the Sermon on the Mount and the parable of the vineyard, undergoes a final conversion. Not being digested into the body of the narrative, the last two or three pages, from an artistic point of view, are, of course, no more than a series of external statements, however true or otherwise Tolstoy's message may be.

The chapters which deal with the political prisoners are chiefly a means of getting across certain ideas to the reader; those dealing with the Henry George single-tax system are more subtle.[18] Politically, all the injustice that Tolstoy is exposing has its origin in the land question, of which Henry George had the solution; but, artistically, this is not as important as

---

[15] Part III, Chs. V, XII, XIII, and XV. [16] Part III, Ch. VI.

[17] Part III, Ch. IV. It is true, however, that Mary Pavlovna questions the platonic nature of his love for Katusha (Part III, Ch. XVII).

[18] Part II, Chs. IV-IX.

Nekhlyudov's relation to that problem as a "repentant noble-man". On the one hand, he makes some appalling discoveries: poverty, even starvation, on his own estate, the death through starvation of his illegitimate child, and the imprisonment of a man who had cut down two of his trees. On the other hand, the peasants show for him their customary respect, and also a deep distrust, which, while it only surprises Nekhlyudov, registers for the reader another aspect of that moral nausea which is contained in the theme of the book. It is inconceivable to them that Nekhlyudov should not be motivated by self-interest and be tricking them in his offer of the land. The conversations with the peasants are distinctly realised:

> 'Then am I to understand that you refuse to take the land?' Nekhlyudov asked, addressing a middle-aged, bare-footed peasant, with a bright look on his face. He was dressed in a tattered coat, and held his worn cap in his left hand in the peculiarly straight position in which soldiers hold theirs when commanded to take them off.
> 'Just so,' said this peasant . . .

There is very little comment; Nekhlyudov is even joyful, in spite of the refusal; but the point has been made dramatically to what extent, in his moral strivings, he is estranged from everyone. The peasants finally accept his offer only when told that "the master" has begun to think of his soul.

3 Revolt against Nature

Nekhlyudov attains a degree of inner clarity early in the story. His conversion in Part I, Chapter xxviii, which gives his activities a fairly definite direction, was brought about by what was initially a vague but strong disgust, a disgust which is wonderfully achieved in the opening chapters, and is potent in him before his visits to the prison, where it reaches its most intensely physical state.

Sordid sexual relations are characteristic of the society in which Nekhlyudov lives. The same in kind as Katusha's history are Nekhlyudov's affairs with Missy and the wife of the *Maréchal de noblesse*, and that of the president of the Court with a Swiss girl.[19] Those who sit in judgment on Maslova suffer

[19] Part I, Chs. II, III, and VI.

Tolstoy's scorn for their limited and self-centred natures as much as for their common guilt. (There is vivid satire here. Matthew Nikitich, the third member of the Court, enters counting the steps he takes, to see if the number is divisible by three, in which case, he imagines, his new treatment will cure his catarrh.[20]) Nekhlyudov is introduced to the reader as a depraved sluggard, typical of his class; and he seduced Katusha, we are told, because, accepting out of weakness the standards of his society, he ceased to believe in his spiritual ego and gave in to the demands of his animal ego. His action is at once an offence against the spirit, and becomes more and more obviously representative, in its social aspects, of the corruption and exploitation of the common people by the upper classes. " 'It happens to everybody—everybody does it,' he said to himself . . .''[21] The repulsive description of the corpse [22] adds to Nekhlyudov's nausea. Shame and physical disgust lead to utter revolt. There is in the best of Tolstoy a profound apprehension of spiritual states through physical sensations. Nekhlyudov's vision of Kolosov and Sophia Vasilyevna as ill-shaped nudes [23] leads up to this:

> There was something very revolting and blasphemous in this representation of his mother as a half-nude beauty. It was all the more disgusting because three months ago, in this very room, lay this same woman, dried up to a mummy, yet filling not only this room, but the whole of the house, with an unbearably disagreeable smell which nothing would overcome.

Tolstoy's dualism lies very deep in *Resurrection*. The whole seduction of Katusha is interpreted in terms of it: Nekhlyudov's conscience was stifled by low animal excitement and the dreadful animal man in him.[24] (But it should be pointed out that this interpretation does not limit the effectiveness of those pages to which it refers, or exhaust their significance. With the imagery of the ice breaking up, the cocks crowing and the dense mist, the sight of Katusha seen through the window, and Nekhlyudov's palpitations, her terror and her physical assent, Chapter XVII of Part I is a profoundly imaginative, truthful, and

[20] Part I, Ch. VII.   [21] Part I, Ch. XVII.   [22] Part I, Ch. XX.
[23] Part I, Ch. XXVII.   [24] Part I, Ch. XVI.

fully accomplished description; and it is in comparison with writing like this that Part III appears so thin.) Then when, after the trial and the evening with the Korchagins, Nekhlyudov understands that his disgust is, at bottom, aversion for himself, the "cleansing of the soul" that follows is the result, we are told, of an awakening in him of the free spiritual being, which is the God within him.

Essential to Tolstoy's dualism is the belief that the dictates of conscience are actually and alone true, and that it is possible for man to attain knowledge of the truth by introspection, if only he can free himself from distractions. For example, a boy is represented as "having it straight from God" that the convicts are just the same kind of people as himself and like everyone else, whereas his sister, under the influence of their parents, decides that they are not, but are bad people who ought to be punished.[25] If only people would believe themselves and have the courage to act by that belief, all would be well.

The inadequacy of this faith has already been suggested; here one should note its relation to Tolstoy's distrust of man's animal nature, for it is that nature which creates the need for distraction. Nekhlyudov had found it too difficult to live believing himself, since, doing so, one has to decide almost every question against one's animal ego. Accordingly there are, in *Resurrection*, frequent representations of people resorting to distractions to quieten their consciences. When Maslova smokes or drinks vodka,[26] one remembers the theory formulated in the essay *Why Do Men Stupefy Themselves?* The General in Siberia became an alcoholic for the same reason.[27] But alcohol and tobacco are not the only distractions. Selenin and the kindly prison inspector could not carry on with their cruel occupations if they did not deceive themselves with regard to the Orthodox Church; and Maslennikov is represented as being so distracted by his wife's "at home" as to be unable to give Nekhlyudov the attention he requires.[28]

When Nekhlyudov is with Maslova in the prison, she purposely thinks of him, not as the young man she had loved, but

[25] Part II, Ch. xxxv.   [26] Part I, Chs. xxix, xxxi, xlvi, and xlviii.
[27] Part III, Ch. xxii.   [28] Part I, Ch. lviii.

as a prostitute's client, in order to protect herself from the memory of a joyful past which his presence in the prison at first awakened in her. Her depravity in this scene is, therefore, comparable to "that dreadful veil" which had been hiding from Nekhlyudov the true nature of his sin. "This woman is dead", thinks Nekhlyudov, and her depravity arouses in him "the tempter", which is but the voice of the animal ego. One form of distraction encourages another. The sequence of cause and effect that then threatens to develop—in which one is guided by consideration of what is practical and of the consequences of one's actions—can only be prevented by intervention from the inner world. Nekhlyudov prays: he must awaken her soul through God.[29]

The relationship that grows up between Katusha and Nekhlyudov is not simple, though underlying it there is a simple dualistic principle, which is stated as being the ultimate truth of the situation. The Tolstoyan sense of reality, however, makes one feel the ambivalence of Nekhlyudov's attempt.

> 'You want to save yourself through me,' she continued. . . . 'You've got pleasure out of me in this life, and want to save yourself through me in the life to come. You are disgusting to me—your spectacles and the whole of your dirty fat mug . . .'[30]

Nekhlyudov is motivated in part, in his highly moral action, by "self-admiration" and "vicious obstinacy".[31]

Yet for all the truthfulness of parts of the book, because Tolstoy assumes the attitude of omniscience, *Resurrection* is a one-sided work: the author takes sides in the struggle it portrays, being a partisan of the spirit. It is as if the revolt in Nekhlyudov of spirit against animal nature were the absolute law of life, as such a revolt is in formal Tolstoyan philosophy.

Nekhlyudov's judgments are, of course, conditioned by the situation in which he is placed: he is a sinner discovering the nature and consequences of his guilt, and his chief sin was his

[29] Part I, Ch. XLIII.

[30] Part I, Ch. XLVIII. Axelrod quotes this passage and remarks that here the preacher in Tolstoy gave way to the artist, and Katusha is right. Of course, but the novel goes on. Axelrod's error consists in thinking that Nekhlyudov has only the motive that Katusha says he has.

[31] Part I, Ch. XLIX, and Part II, Ch. XXIX.

seduction of Katusha, so that it is not surprising that his remorse should give rise to a negative attitude towards sex. But,
as regards sex, his nausea has no limit. When he is revolted
by the refined, hypocritical Mariette and by the sight of a
common prostitute, he makes a judgment which, it seems, the
reader is to accept without qualification.

> The animalism of the brute nature in man is disgusting, but
> as long as it remains in its naked form we observe it from the
> height of our spiritual life and despise it. . . .[32]

Tolstoy is unable to place this judgment as a product of
Nekhlyudov's psychological condition, but treats it as final.

Further evidence that this is so is provided by the shocking
association of the attitudes of Katusha and the virgin, Mary
Pavlovna:

> They were also united by the repulsion both felt from sexual love.
> The one loathed that love, having experienced all its horrors;
> the other, never having experienced it, looked on it as some-
> thing incomprehensible, and at the same time as something
> repugnant and offensive to human dignity.[33]

There is nothing in the book to modify this view, not even
Simonson's religious teaching, which is something like "reverence for life".

And it is not in regard to sexual love alone that *Resurrection*
is one-sided, for the denial of any beauty in sex cannot be considered in isolation from the feelings Tolstoy expresses in the
book about the whole beauty of the natural world and human
life; and here joy is blended with regret, with the melancholy
of renunciation, and a failure in creativity.

The novel begins with appreciation of a spring morning,
the aggressive tones suggesting that man's sin consists in his
being out of harmony with nature:

> It was not this spring morning men thought sacred and worthy
> of consideration, not the beauty of God's world, given for a joy
> to all creatures—this beauty which inclines the heart to peace,
> to harmony, and to love—but only their own devices for en-
> slaving one another.

[32] Part II, Ch. xxviii.   [33] Part III, Ch. iii.

L

Consistent with this feeling is the admiration for the footman Philip, part of whose superiority to his mistress, Sophia Vasilyevna, and to Kolosov, consists in the fact that he is broadchested, muscular, and handsome. His physical development serves to emphasise by contrast the perverted quality of their culture. Similar admiration is expressed in a touching description of a convict, whose death comes as the climax of Part II:

> He was a man in the full bloom of life. Notwithstanding the disfigurement from half of his head being shaved, the straight, though not high forehead, slightly arched above the black, lifeless eyes, was very fine, and so was the nose above the thin, black moustache. There was a smile on the lips that were already growing blue. . . .
> One could see that possibilities of a higher life had been destroyed in this man, while the fine bones of his hands and shackled feet, the strong muscles of all his well-proportioned limbs, showed what a beautiful, strong, agile human animal he had been.[34]

This passage is remarkable, not only for the pity it reveals (in this respect it is but a development of what has gone before), but also because, by the very dualism it contains, it shows clearly how that pity is aroused, in spite of Tolstoyan theory, by reverence for the animal personality; and hence it implies that, like Hadji Murad and the "Tartar" thistle that symbolises him, this convict had a right to bodily life merely by virtue of what he was in himself, or of what he was as a work of nature, quite apart from any function that might be required of his personality as a tool of the spirit.

But when Tolstoy examines the causes that led to this death, his dualism appears in its familiar light. When Nekhlyudov reflects on the incident, after finding, in a passage reminiscent of *War and Peace*, that none of the officials concerned is individually guilty, he decides that their error consists in supposing that there are circumstances under which one can act in disregard of the eternal law of love written by God in the hearts of men.[35] The spirit is vindicated as the ground of love, the officials being

[34] Part II, Ch. XXXVII.   [35] Part II, Ch. XL.

distracted from it by the obligations of their office. Being impermeable to the feelings of humanity, they are against nature; but their restoration lies in the resurrection of the spirit. What is, on the face of it, an opposition of pity and indifference becomes, in Tolstoy's eyes, a struggle between the animal and the spirit. Goodness has no external cause, so that the sight of suffering cannot of itself create spiritual compassion; and animal pity is inadequate, for the absolute devotion which is required as the solution of our ills is only possible if the animal ego is flooded by the spiritual.[36] One inevitably asks, therefore, what value the animal ego and the natural world, of which it is a part, will have in the order of things that will obtain when the resurrection of the spirit is complete, seeing that nausea at the mutilation of that world is a necessary concomitant in Nekhlyudov's resurrection.

The novel contains no answer to this question; and hence its tragic incompleteness. Nekhlyudov's boyish, pure love for Katusha, which was symbolised by the kiss behind the lilac bush, was, for all its concentration upon her, a part of his joy in life as a whole—a joy which is seen to be legitimate only so long as the spiritual ego predominates.[37] For on the last page of the book, Nekhlyudov comes to think that our sin consists in our imagining that life is given us for our own enjoyment and that we, and not God, are the masters of our lives. Before Nekhlyudov, at the close, is a career of endless submission to God's will, without there being any sight of the benefit that men's natural lives may ultimately receive. The fault is not only that, in Tolstoy's interpretation, the five commandments are all negative, or that, as Aylmer Maude complains,[38] we never know what occupation Nekhlyudov will choose, but also that there is no artistically embodied vision of what the material

---

[36] The distinction between "spiritual compassion" and "animal pity" is Tolstoy's: "At a certain stage in his spiritual development, a man should refrain from intensifying in himself the feeling of personal pity for another being. This feeling in itself is animal, and in a sensitive man it is always present in sufficient strength without its being artificially kindled. Rather, he should encourage spiritual compassion in himself. The soul of someone I love should always be dearer to me than his body." *Ripe Ears*, quoted by Plekhanov in "A Confusion of Ideas", I, *L. N. Tolstoy v russkoy kritike*, ed. S. P. Bychkov.

[37] Part I, Ch. XII.

[38] *The Life of Tolstoy*, Vol. II, Ch. XV.

results of his spiritual labours will be. The cry is for forgiveness, and for a return to the land; yet there is no realisation of
the satisfaction of a life of labour—apart from that at the close
of Part II, when Nekhlyudov mixes with a crowd of workmen
in the train, and feels in the occasion the possibilities of "a
new, unknown, and beautiful world". The tragedy is that this
world is never explored; indeed, Part III takes us away from
it. Moreover, the joy of that kiss behind the lilac bush is never
rediscovered. Recalling "chains, shaven heads, fighting and
debauchery, the dying Kriltsov, Katusha and the whole of her
past", Nekhlyudov envies the General's daughter her happiness
in her children.[39] And, when he sees Katusha after that, "I
want to live, I want a family, children, I want a human life,"
are the thoughts that flash through his mind.[40] But it is not to
be, and the renunciation is not just Nekhlyudov's. The message
of the novel is summed up in the words of the saintly old man in
Chapters XXI and XXVII of Part III: he is a symbol of spiritual
self-possession, and a believer in the possibility of spiritual
unity, but he sees no end to renunciation. "I have given up
everything," he says, expecting nothing, ". . . and it is not
possible to offend me."

He protests, however, against "the seal of Antichrist":

> Men should eat bread in the sweat of their brow. But *he* has
> locked them up with no work to do, and feeds them like swine,
> so that they should turn into beasts.

Evidently man's spiritual life is not independent of his material
conditions; the prison system may degrade or destroy the spirit.
If the personality has to flourish, though beneath Adam's curse,
before the spirit can be exalted, then the two are vitally interrelated, and Tolstoy's dualism is false. Certainly, when the
beauties of the external world and of the human personality
are realised as they are, in occasional flashes, in *Resurrection*,
the protest should not preclude vindication of them. At one
point in the story Nekhlyudov remembers a hunting expedi-
tion, and his recollections end with this:

> All this comes back to Nekhlyudov's mind, but, above all, the
> joyous sense of health, strength, and freedom from care: the

[39] Part III, Ch. xxiv.   [40] Part III, Ch. xxv.

lungs breathing in the frosty air so deeply that the fur cloak is drawn tightly on his chest; the fine snow dropping from the low branches on to his face; his body warm, his face fresh, and his soul free from care, self-reproach, fear, or desire. . . . How beautiful it was. And now, O God! what torment, what trouble![41]

Coming as it does when Nekhlyudov is leaving the prison, this reminiscence heightens by contrast the reader's sense of horror at the world of victims and judges—it recalls what they are deprived of, especially the fine sensuousness of communion with nature. By associating a clear conscience with the enjoyment of nature, it suggests that there is now a gulf separating Nekhlyudov from the chance of such enjoyment. But Tolstoy adds that Nekhlyudov's soul at that time, besides being free from self-reproach, was free from desire, and the allying of that condition with the joyous sense of health and strength is significant. *Resurrection* is not only an assault on man's greed, stupidity, hypocrisy, and indifference, but also a revolt against the enormity of his desires; and the satisfaction of desire is not generally seen as compatible with peaceful and just human relations. The problem, to Tolstoy, is to subdue desires by the spirit, and not to try to recognise them as part of that nature which is a source of joy.

Tolstoy has been accused of hating beauty. He was indeed hostile to it in theory, as the following shows:

Beauty is nothing but what pleases us. The notion of beauty not only does not coincide with goodness, but rather is contrary to it; for the good most often coincides with victory over the passions while beauty is at the root of our passions.[42]

His sense of guilt, and his horror at the wickedness of the "perverted" society to which he belonged, while making him wish for a simpler and more "natural" way of life, caused him also to turn in disgust from all those animal desires which are in any way dangerous. Believing in some ideal natural state, he attempted to distinguish between what was natural and what was perverted; but in the end the activity only of man's divine

[41] Part I, Ch. XLIX.
[42] *What is Art?*, VII. Alymer Maude puts these words in a footnote to his translation, saying that Tolstoy finally deleted them.

essence was sanctioned. Though recognising and able to re-create the beauty of the external world and the personality, Tolstoy could not finally relate it to man's best aspirations. He felt that such a relation had existed in the past and was nostalgic for it, but was able to recapture it only fleetingly.

Back on the estate inherited from his aunts, Nekhlyudov, one warm thundery night, can escape for a while from the burden of his guilt, and recall the happy memories of that place. There is a marvellous evocation of the night: the air fragrant with the scent of young birch leaves, the murmur of water from the mill, the songs of nightingales and the cackle of geese, the rising moon, sheet lightning illumining the dilapidated house and over-grown garden, and thunder in the distance; then the first cock-crowing begins:

> There is a saying that if the cocks crow early the night will be a merry one. For Nekhlyudov the night was more than merry: it was a happy, joyful night. Imagination renewed the impressions of the happy summer he had spent here as an innocent lad, and he felt himself as he had been, not only then but at all the best moments of his life. He not only remembered, but felt as he had felt when, at the age of fourteen, he prayed that God would show him the truth. . . .[43]

But the possibility of stabilising that relation, of completing the reconciliation of the sense of natural beauty with the inward striving for perfection, is overlooked in the novel. The revolt against the state of the oppressed gives rise to a demand for unlimited self-abnegation, inconsistent with the call to a more natural way of living, which should comprise defence of the passionate side of man, homage to Dionysus. Tolstoy's awareness of sin and suffering was so great that he could harmonise nothing else with it; and lost in the pity for the oppressed, and in the shame that pity provokes, is an adequate sense of what they deserve, of the beauty of which they are wickedly deprived.

[43] Part II, Ch. VIII.

Select Bibliography

Tolstoy's works, including his diaries and letters, have been published in Moscow in a monumental edition of ninety volumes, *Polnoe sobranie sochineny*, under the general editorship of V. G. Chertkov (Gosizdat) 1928–58. This edition gives details of the composition and first publication of Tolstoy's works.

Louise and Aylmer Maude's translations have been published by the Oxford University Press in the twenty-one volume Tolstoy Centenary Edition (London, 1928–37), together with *The Life of Tolstoy*, and in the World's Classics series (London, 1906–40), in which they are now available in sixteen volumes.

Another edition of Tolstoy in English is Leo Wiener's *The Complete Works of Count Tolstoy* (24 vols.), London (Dent), 1904–5. This includes a "Bibliography of Works and Articles on Tolstoy in English, German, and French".

There is a concise *Bibliografichesky ukazatel' tvoreny L. N. Tolstogo*, compiled by A. L. Bem, Leningrad (Academy of Sciences of U.S.S.R.), 1926.

Readers may wish to consult the following:

Bitovt, Yu. Yu. *Graf L. Tolstoy v literature i iskusstve.* Moscow (Sytin) 1903.

Shelyapina, N. G., and others. *Bibliografiya literatury o L. N. Tolstom 1917–1958.* Moscow (Vsesoyuznaya knizhnaya palata) 1960.

——. *Bibliografiya literatury o L. N. Tolstom 1959–1961.* Moscow ("Kniga") 1965.

There is a useful select bibliography, together with a note on recent Russian work on Tolstoy, in Theodore Redpath's *Tolstoy*, London (Bowes & Bowes), 1960.

I. TOLSTOY'S WORKS

1. SKETCHES, STORIES, AND NOVELS

Childhood, in *Sovremennik*, Vol. xxxv, 1852.
The Raid, op. cit., Vol. xxxviii, 1853.
Boyhood, op. cit., Vol. xlvii, 1854.
Recollections of a Billiard-Marker, op. cit., Vol. xlix, 1855.
Sevastopol in December, op. cit., Vol. li, 1855.
Sevastopol in May, op. cit., Vol. liii, 1855.
The Wood-Felling, op. cit., Vol. liii, 1855.
Sevastopol in August, op. cit., Vol. lv, 1856.
The Snow Storm, op. cit., Vol. lvi, 1856.

Two Hussars, op. cit., Vol. LVII, 1856.
Meeting a Moscow Acquaintance in the Detachment (Reduced to the Ranks), in *Biblioteka dlya Chteniya,* Vol. CXL, 1856.
A Landlord's Morning, in *Otechestvennye Zapiski,* Vol. CIX, 1856.
Youth, in *Sovremennik,* Vol. LXI, 1857.
Lucerne, op. cit., Vol. LXV, 1857.
Albert, op. cit., Vol. LXX, 1858.
Three Deaths, in *Biblioteka dlya Chteniya,* Vol. CLIII, 1859.
Family Happiness, in *Russky Vestnik,* Vol. XX, 1859.
The Cossacks, op. cit., Vol. XLIII, 1863.
Polikushka, op. cit., Vol. XLIII, 1863.
1805 (Parts I and II of *War and Peace*), *op. cit.,* Vol. LV, 1865, and Vols. LXI and LXII, 1866.
War and Peace. (6 vols.) Moscow (Ris) 1868–9.
A Prisoner in the Caucasus, in *Zarya,* 1872.
God Sees the Truth, in *Beseda,* 1872.
Anna Karenina, Parts I–VII, in *Russky Vestnik,* Vols. CXV and CXVI, 1875, Vols. CXXI, CXXII, and CXXVI, 1876, and Vols. CXXVII and CXXVIII, 1877; Part VIII, Moscow (Ris) 1877.
What Men Live By, in *Detsky Otdykh,* 1881.
The Decembrists, in *XXV Years: 1859–1884,* Petersburg, 1884.
Where Love is, God is, in *Posrednik,* 1886.
A Spark Neglected Burns the House, op. cit., 1886.
Two Old Men, op. cit., 1886.
The Story of Ivan the Fool, op. cit., 1886.
How Much Land Does a Man Need?, in *Russkoe Bogatstvo,* 1886.
The Three Hermits, in *Niva,* 1886.
The Candle, in *Knizhki Nedeli,* 1886.
The Godson, in *Knizhka Nedeli,* 1886.
Kholstomer (the story of a horse), in *Sochineniya grafa L. N. Tolstogo* (5th ed.), Vol. III, Moscow, 1886.
The Death of Ivan Ilych, in *Sochineniya,* Part XII, Moscow, 1886.
The Kreutzer Sonata. Berlin (Ber) 1890.
Emelyan and the Empty Drum. Geneva (Elpidine) 1891.
Walk in the Light While There is Light. Geneva (Elpidine) 1892.
Master and Man, in *Severny Vestnik,* 1895.
Resurrection, in *Niva,* 1899.
The Restoration of Hell. Christchurch, Hants. (Izdanie "Svobodnogo Slova") 1903.
Three Days in the Country, in *Vestnik Evropy,* 1910.

Posthumous

ed. V. G. Chertkov

The Devil. Moscow (A. L. Tolstaya) 1911.
Father Sergius. Moscow (A. L. Tolstaya) 1911.
After the Ball. Moscow (A. L. Tolstaya) 1911.

The Forged Coupon. Moscow (A. L. Tolstaya) 1911.
Alësha Gorshok. Moscow (A. L. Tolstaya) 1911.
What I Dreamt. Moscow (A. L. Tolstaya) 1911.
The Wisdom of Children. Moscow (A. L. Tolstaya) 1911.
No One in the World is Guilty. Moscow (A. L. Tolstaya) 1911.
The Memoirs of a Madman. Moscow (A. L. Tolstaya) 1912.
Hadji Murad. Berlin (Ladyzhnikov) 1912.
Posthumous Memoirs of the Hermit, Fëdor Kuzmich. Berlin ("Svobodnoe Slovo") 1912.

2. PLAYS

The First Distiller, in *Posrednik,* 1886.
The Power of Darkness, in *Sochineniya* (6th ed.), Moscow, 1886.
The Fruits of Enlightenment, in *In Memory of S. A. Yuryev,* Moscow, 1890.

Posthumous
ed. V. G. Chertkov

The Light Shines in Darkness. Moscow (A. L. Tolstaya) 1911.
The Cause of it All. Moscow (A. L. Tolstaya) 1911.
The Live Corpse. Moscow (A. L. Tolstaya) 1912.

3. MISCELLANIES, ETC.

ABC Book. Petersburg (Tipografiya Zamyslovskogo) 1872.
New ABC Book. Moscow (Tip. Tarletskogo i Terikhova) 1875.
Russian Readers. Moscow (Ris) 1875.
A Circle of Reading (including the stories *What For?, Divine and Human,* and *Korney Vasilyev*). Moscow (*Posrednik*) 1906.
For Every Day, in *Knizhnaya Letopis'* and *Novaya Rus',* 1909–10.

Posthumous
The Path of Life. Moscow (*Posrednik*) 1911.

4. ARTICLES AND TREATISES

Yasnaya Polyana (magazine), 1862.
On Popular Education, in *Otechestvennye Zapiski,* Vol. CCXVI, 1874.
Confession. Geneva (Elpidine) 1884.
What I Believe. Moscow (Kushnerev) 1884.
What Then Must We Do?, in *Sochineniya,* Part XII, Moscow, 1886.
On Life, in *Sochineniya,* Part XIII, Moscow, 1888.
The Gospel in Brief. Geneva (Elpidine) 1890.
A Criticism of Dogmatic Theology. Geneva (Elpidine) 1891.
Why Do Men Stupefy Themselves?, preface to P. S. Alexeev's *On Drunkenness.* Moscow (*Russkaya Mysl'*) 1891.

The First Step, in *Voprosy Filosofii i Psikhologii*, 1892.
On Hunger, in English in *The Daily Telegraph*, 1892.
Harmony and Translation of the Four Gospels. Geneva (Elpidine) Vol. I, 1892;
   Vol. II, 1893; Vol. III, 1894.
Non-Acting, in *Severny Vestnik*, 1893.
The Kingdom of God is Within You. Berlin (Deibner) 1893–4.
Religion and Morality, in German, Berlin, 1894.
"Preface", to Guy de Maupassant's *Mont-Oriol*, translated by L. P. Niki-
   forov. Moscow (*Posrednik*) 1894.
Christianity and Patriotism. Geneva (Elpidine) 1895.
What is Art?, in *Voprosy Filosofii i Psikhologii*, 1897–8.
"Preface", to a translation of Edward Carpenter's *Modern Science*, in
   Severny Vestnik, 1898.
The Christian Teaching. Purleigh, Essex (V. G. Chertkov) 1898.
The Slavery of Our Times. Purleigh ("Svobodnoe Slovo") 1900.
Patriotism and Government, in *Listki Svobodnogo Slova*, 1900.
A Reply to the Synod's Edict, op. cit., 1901.
What is Religion?. Christchurch ("Svobodnoe Slovo") 1902.
"Preface", to W. von Polenz's *Der Büttnerbauer*, translated by V. Velichkina.
   Moscow (*Posrednik*) 1902.
An Appeal to the Clergy. Christchurch ("Svobodnoe Slovo") 1903.
Bethink Yourselves! (on the Russo-Japanese War). Christchurch ("Svobod-
   noe Slovo") 1904.
The End of the Century. Christchurch ("Svobodnoe Slovo") 1905.
A Great Iniquity, in *Russkaya Mysl'*, 1905.
On the Meaning of the Russian Revolution, in *Posrednik*, 1906.
Shakespeare and the Drama, in *Russkoe Slovo*, 1906.
Believe Yourselves, op. cit., 1907.
I Cannot Be Silent, in *Slovo*, 1908.
The Teaching of Christ. Moscow (*Posrednik*) 1908.
The Law of Violence and the Law of Love. Christchurch ("Svobodnoe Slovo")
   1909.
On Science, in *Russkie Vedomosti*, 1909.

Posthumous

An Inevitable Revolution, in *Sochineniya* (12th ed.), Moscow, 1911.

II. BIOGRAPHICAL STUDIES

ASQUITH, LADY CYNTHIA. *Married to Tolstoy.* London (Hutchinson) 1960.
BEHRS, S. A. *Recollections of Count Leo Tolstoy*, translated by C. E. Turner.
   London (Heinemann) 1893.
BIRYUKOV, P. I. *L. N. Tolstoy: biografiya* (3 vols.). Berlin (Ladyzhnikov)
   1921.
GORKY, MAXIM. *Reminiscences of Tolstoy, Chekhov and Andreev*, translated
   by Katherine Mansfield, S. S. Koteliansky, and Leonard Woolf.
   London (Hogarth) 1934.

GUSEV, N. N. *Lev Nikolaevich Tolstoy: materialy k biografii, s 1828 po 1855 god.* Moscow (Academy of Sciences of U.S.S.R.) 1954.

——. *Lev Nikolaevich Tolstoy: materialy k biografii, s 1855 po 1869 god.* Moscow (Academy of Sciences of U.S.S.R.) 1957.

——. *Lev Nikolaevich Tolstoy: materialy k biografii, s 1870 po 1881 god.* Moscow (Academy of Sciences of U.S.S.R.) 1963.

GUSEV, N. N., and MISHIN, V. S., edd. *L. N. Tolstoy v vospominaniyakh sovremennikov* (2 vols.). Moscow (Gosizdat) 1955.

LEON, DERRICK. *Tolstoy, his Life and Work.* London (Routledge) 1944.

MAUDE, AYLMER. *The Life of Tolstoy* (2 vols. in one). London (Oxford U.P.) 1953.

SIMMONS, E. J. *Leo Tolstoy.* London (Lehmann) 1949.

TOLSTOY, COUNTESS ALEXANDRA. *Tolstoy: A Life of My Father*, translated by E. R. Hapgood. New York (Harper) 1953.

TOLSTOY, COUNT ILYA. *Reminiscences of Tolstoy*, translated by G. Calderson. London (Chapman and Hall) 1914.

TOLSTOY, COUNT SERGEI. *Tolstoy Remembered by his Son*, translated by Moura Budberg. London (Weidenfeld and Nicolson) 1961.

III. CRITICAL STUDIES

ARDENS (APOSTOLOV), N. N. *Tvorchesky put' L. N. Tolstogo.* Moscow (Academy of Sciences of U.S.S.R.) 1962.

ARNOLD, MATTHEW. "Count Leo Tolstoi", in *Essays in Criticism* (second series). London (Macmillan) 1958.

AXELROD, E. L. (L. I.). *Tolstois Weltanschauung und ihre Entwickelung.* Stuttgart (Enke) 1902.

BAYLEY, JOHN. *Tolstoy and the Novel.* London (Chatto and Windus) 1966.

BERLIN, SIR ISAIAH. *The Hedgehog and the Fox: An Essay on Tolstoy's View of History.* New York (Mentor) 1957.

——. "Tolstoy and Enlightenment", in *Encounter*, Vol. XVI (Feb. 1961).

BURSOV, B. I. *Lev Tolstoy i russky roman.* Moscow and Leningrad (Academy of Sciences of U.S.S.R.) 1963.

BYCHKOV, S. P., ed. *L. N. Tolstoy v russkoy kritike, Sbornik statey.* Moscow (Gosizdat) 1960.

CHRISTIAN, R. F. *Tolstoy's 'War and Peace': A Study.* Oxford (Clarendon Press) 1962.

DAVIE, DONALD, ed. *Russian Literature and Modern English Fiction, A Collection of Critical Essays.* Chicago (University of Chicago Press) 1965.

ERMILOV, V. V. *Tolstoy—romanist: "Voyna i mir", "Anna Karenina", "Voskresenie".* Moscow ("Khudozhestvennaya Literatura") 1965.

EYKHENBAUM, B. M. *Molodoy Tolstoy.* Petersburg and Berlin (Grzhebin) 1922.

——. *Lev Tolstoy, Book I, 50-ye gody.* Leningrad ("Priboy") 1928.

——. *Lev Tolstoy, Book II, 60-ye gody.* Moscow and Leningrad (Goslitizdat) 1931.

EYKHENBAUM, B. M. *Lev Tolstoy, 70-ye gody*, ed. B. I. Bursov. Leningrad (Sovetsky pisatel') 1960.

FLEW, ANTONY. "Tolstoi and the Meaning of Life", in *Ethics*, Vol. LXXIII (Jan. 1963).

FRICHE, V. M., ed. *O Tolstom: Literaturno-kritichesky sbornik*. Moscow and Leningrad (Gosizdat) 1928.

HOWELLS, W. D. *Criticism and Fiction, and Other Essays*. New York (New York University Press) 1959.

KHRAPCHENKO, M. B. *Lev Tolstoy kak khudozhnik*. Moscow (Sovetsky pisatel') 1963.

LAVRIN, JANKO. *Tolstoy: A Psycho-critical Study*. London (Collins) 1924.

——. *Tolstoy: An Approach*. London (Methuen) 1944.

LEONTIEV, K. N. *O romanakh gr. L. N. Tolstogo: Kritichesky etyud*. Moscow 1911.

LOMUNOV, K. N. *Dramaturgiya L. N. Tolstogo*. Moscow (Gosizdat) 1956.

LUBBOCK, PERCY. *The Craft of Fiction*. London (Smith) 1921.

LUKÁCS, GEORGE. "Tolstoy and the Development of Realism", in *Studies in European Realism*, translated by Edith Bone. London (Hillway) 1950.

MANN, THOMAS. *Goethe und Tolstoi: zum Problem der Humanität*. Berlin (Fischer) 1932.

MEREZHKOVSKY, D. S. *Tolstoi as Man and Artist, with an Essay on Dosto-ievski*. London (Constable) 1902.

MIRSKY, PRINCE D. S. *Contemporary Russian Literature, 1881–1925*. London (Routledge) 1926.

——. *A History of Russian Literature, from the Earliest Times to the Death of Dostoyevsky, 1881*. London (Routledge) 1927.

MYSHKOVSKAYA, L. M. *Masterstvo L. N. Tolstogo*. Moscow (Sovetsky pisatel') 1958.

NOYES, G. R. *Tolstoy*. London (Murray) 1919.

PLAKHOTISHINA, V. T. *Khudozhestvennoe masterstvo L. N. Tolstogo v romane "Voskresenie"*. Kiev (Kiev State University) 1958.

RAHV, PHILIP. "Tolstoy: the Green Twig and the Black Trunk", in *Image and Idea, Twenty Essays on Literary Themes*. Norfolk, Conn. (New Directions) 1957.

REDPATH, THEODORE. *Tolstoy*. London (Bowes & Bowes) 1960.

ROLLAND, ROMAIN. *Vie de Tolstoi*. Paris (Librairie Hachette) 1919.

SIMMONS, E. J. *Introduction to Russian Realism*. Bloomington (Indiana University Press) 1965.

STEINER, GEORGE. *Tolstoy or Dostoevsky: An Essay in Contrast*. London (Faber) 1959.

STRUVE, GLEB. "Tolstoy in Soviet Criticism", in *The Russian Review*, Vol. XIX (April 1960).

VOGÜÉ, E. M. DE. *Le Roman Russe*. Paris (Librairie Plon) 1886.

WEISBEIN, NICOLAS. *L'Évolution Religieuse de Tolstoi*. Paris (Librairie des Cinq Continents) 1960.

WOODCOCK, GEORGE. *Anarchism: A History of Libertarian Ideas and Movements*. Harmondsworth (Penguin) 1963.

ZELINSKY, V. A. *Russkaya kriticheskaya literatura o proizvedeniyakh L. N. Tolstogo* (7 vols.). Moscow 1888–1902.

ZHDANOV, V. A. *Tvorcheskaya istoriya "Anny Kareninoy": materialy i nablyudeniya.* Moscow (Sovetsky pisatel') 1957.

——. *Tvorcheskaya istoriya romana L. N. Tolstogo "Voskresenie": materialy i nablyudeniya.* Moscow (Sovetsky pisatel') 1960.

Index